LEARNING TO LIVE
An American Story

James W. H. Sell

ARCHWAY
PUBLISHING

Archway Publishing books may be ordered through booksellers or by contacting:

Archway Publishing
1663 Liberty Drive
Bloomington, IN 47403
www.archwaypublishing.com
1 (888) 242-5904

Because of the dynamic nature of the Internet, any web addresses or
links contained in this book may have changed since publication and
may no longer be valid. The views expressed in this work are solely those
of the author and do not necessarily reflect the views of the publisher,
and the publisher hereby disclaims any responsibility for them.

Any people depicted in stock imagery provided by Thinkstock are models,
and such images are being used for illustrative purposes only.
Certain stock imagery © Thinkstock.

ISBN: 978-1-4808-1546-9 (sc)
ISBN: 978-1-4808-1547-6 (hc)
ISBN: 978-1-4808-1548-3 (e)

Library of Congress Control Number: 2015902851

Print information available on the last page.

Archway Publishing rev. date: 02/23/2015

With love, I dedicate this book to

Ellen Major Sell, James Andrew and Neelam Sell,
Kathryn Sell Garcia and Christian Garcia Fuentes,
Aakash William Sell, Roshan James Sell, Elena Coco
Garcia, Raina Olivia Sell and Marco Gael Garcia.

CONTENTS

PREFACE

This is the story of my journey through the ordained ministry of the Episcopal Church. It was a life that suited my values and personality like no other. It began when the norms and standards of institutional religion fueled American culture in the late 1950s and early 1960s. Theologians like Reinhold Niebuhr and Karl Barth were instructing both religious and political thinkers. Karl Jung's books were read by both the psychoanalyst and the pastoral counselor. Billy Graham could be quoted to score points with both the voter and the person in the pew. In short, public religion had a place at just about every table. I was one of about five or six from my high school class to be ordained, including four into the Episcopal Church. Also, I had four other college mates who became ordained Episcopalians as well.

However, from the time of my ordination in 1969 up until the present moment, we have observed a constant pattern of decline in worship life in international and American churches. At the beginning, the decline was just a trickle, somewhat offset by the growth of certain evangelical groups. Today, almost all denominations and faiths are retracting into uncertain futures. The buffet of delightful things to do on a Sunday in lieu of worship is a feast for the body, mind, heart, and spirit. There is no longer any relationship between a person having a spiritual identity and claiming responsible citizenship. In other words, attendance at worship simply does not matter in the public dialogue. We in the church, synagogue, and mosque have been gently invited to surrender our seats at that proverbial dining table.

But I am nothing if I am not hopeful. To be a Christian is to live with a sense that resurrections are at the core of every history. Looking at the past fifty years of church life might help us to see how we have arrived at these present transformational moments.

I am sure the church of the in-breaking future will be so fundamentally different from its recent past that it will be hard to imagine for many of us. But hold on—it will have its antecedents. Like a phrase from a commercial for Kellogg's Corn Flakes, we will "taste it again for the very first time." I think those advertising authors must have had T. S. Eliot on their minds.

> We shall not cease from exploration
> And the end of all our exploring
> Will be to arrive where we started
> And know the place for the first time.[1]

In real ways, I think we are ready to return to our most ancient roots, where, on the fragile edge of society, we became a steady pathway to an abundant life and, ultimately, the driving force for liberation and justice. I believe the Christians who are much like contemporary Episcopalians will be the harbingers of that future. Those who have taken the most compelling

---

[1] T. S. Eliot's "Little Gidding" from *Four Quartets*, (Harcourt Brace& Co.) published in the month of my birth in 1942.

stands for human integrity and inclusivity in recent history without losing their sacred core will be the bearers of America's spiritual reawakening. When the time is ripe, that reawakening will usher in something far more authentic than anything we have ever experienced before. Deep in our spirits, we know that these qualities are the very substance of what all people were created to be from the beginning.

INTRODUCTION

Do you realize that more than three thousand American churches from all denominations close their doors every year? That is just about nine churches a day. This number includes little rural midwestern Methodist churches, inner-city store front Baptist churches, ethnically connected Roman Catholic and Lutheran churches, nondenominational churches that cropped up in the South at the time of the integration of schools, and, yes, plenty of Episcopal congregations whose members have grown older and drifted off into heaven. Is anyone surprised? If you drive through any town in America, you will see "For Sale" signs in front of all kinds of church properties.

But deep in the heart of the King James Version of Hebrew scripture are five compelling words that could serve as a banner to spread across the front of those closed churches: "Without a vision the people perish."[2] I have been to a number of churches that have no vision and are just waiting for their turn to lock the doors and turn off the lights.

You can spot one within seconds - maybe before you even walk in the door. Such churches display a lack of vigor and enthusiasm and an inability to get a handle on the situation. All too often, I have sat through a service, stood up, walked

---

[2] Proverbs 29:18.

out (certainly, no one ever hounded me to stay in such a place), and thought to myself, *Why in God's name does anyone come here? Why do people waste a perfectly lovely Sunday morning in this depressing church?* In the eyes of the people, I saw despair, boredom, and futility. In one such example, the worship was rote, the music was flat, and the preaching was tired. In another, the worship looked as if it came out of the 1950s, the music was contrived,[3] and the preaching sounded as if it came from a textbook. One gets a feeling that in most of these dying institutions, the clergyperson views his or her ministry as nothing more than a gentle custodial presence. Their chief activity is to care for the elderly at the end of their lives. When there is no vision, people cannot grasp what their parish should embody. And please God, I trust that the younger members will not die physically; however, they will die spiritually and simply walk away - not with a bang, but with nary a whimper either.

Total church attendance is currently decreasing by one percentage point per year. At this rate, an institution that has flourished for two thousand years could be completely out of business in less than one hundred years. The erosion we have all observed in the institutional church has some significant roots in the failure of some of its leadership. Billy Graham was probably the last nationally known preacher. Martin Luther King Jr. was the last major ordained leader. While celebrities and heroes like them were gifts to us, we need something far more basic today.

---

[3] What I call the "Dominique effect" after the 1960s French folk guitar piece by the so-called Singing Nun, Jeanine Deckers (a.k.a. Soeur Sourire, or Sister Smile).

We need visionaries! We need prophets! We need deeply intelligent theologians who can bring wisdom and integrity to spiritual quests. We need wise women and men who can articulate the simple gifts of the Christian faith with clear, compelling vulnerability and unpretentious transparency. We need bishops and a church hierarchy that will set the example for hard work, creativity, courage and wisdom. They cannot let mediocrity and banality invade their clergy and congregations.

Finally, there is only one reason for any church to exist: to help its members grow into spiritual beings, equipped to discern authentic religion from the inane nonsense offered up by people trying to corner the theological market with half-baked schemes. Rather than offer spiritual connectivity, they act as purveyors of the wildest array of placebos they can find. Those range from crushing fundamentalism and narrow-minded scare tactics to the imitation of religion personified by isolating cult-like fringe groups; from trendy pop cultures to intellectual mind games; from a failure to be honest with people's fragile souls to psychosexual dysfunction that has already obliterated a whole generation of prospective seekers.

Many churches now have entire congregations that have grown up with almost no exposure to effective, attractive church life - and those churches are running on empty. When they finally sputter out of gas, they will surely die as well.

What is our vision? What commands our allegiance, our faith, and our respect? Why do we exist, and what are we called to be? First and foremost, we are to be a place for the nurture of an individual's personal spiritual growth. A church is the place for the shaping of our souls. It is not a service club, a rock concert, a bingo parlor, or a debating society. It is a place of prayer, healing, spiritual friendship, sharing, discernment, hope, learning, celebration and forgiveness. It is about honoring every journey by believing that God deals uniquely and appropriately with each of us. It is about being radically inclusive and obsessively loving. It is about the Eucharist and life and death. It is the home of baptisms, weddings, burials, Christmas, Easter, Pentecost and homecomings - and coming home.

When any church grabs that simple vision with passion and creativity, something unbelievable will happen. If they stay glued to it, they will have to tear down their walls and pave over their lawns, because people will insist that they be allowed to join in.

It is counterproductive to rely on canned sermons and programs on the one hand or oppressive rigidity on the other. To be an alive and lively family of God, all any congregation needs to do is take advantage of the obvious resources it has always had available to it. Churches need to rediscover and relearn those things that make our spiritual lives legitimate, personal, and meaningful. They need to be steeped in the love of Christianity. They must hold in their hearts the empowerment of worship, the enrichment of learning, the blessing of service, the pleasures of giving, the joy of evangelism, and the transformation of outreach. They must be welcoming and compassionate. They must be willing to speak straightforwardly to those who seek to compromise justice with arrogance, deceit, or self-aggrandizement.

In Deuteronomy, Moses says to the people of Israel, "I have set before you today life and prosperity, death and adversity. Choose life."[4]

The vision of American Christianity is on the table. We must choose life and spiritual revitalization. Churches are always in the midst of God's eternally ongoing reconstruction phase. But right now, we are seeing the largest re-creation of the Christian enterprise since the Reformation. Worldwide Christianity is shrinking into a small body of active worshipers for the moment, but the ministry of Jesus Christ is not going away. If it is authentic at its very heart, it is here to stay forever. Keep your eye on the new Pope, Francis. Unlike any major spokesperson in years, he seems to behold the vision. As we evolve into a more inclusive, open-minded body that is truly in touch with the enlightenment of the Holy Spirit, we will come back with a credibility and effectiveness that we have not known in our lifetimes.

Something really remarkable is in the late stages of the last trimester before birth. As one startling example, over the past fifty years, I have watched the Episcopal Church transform itself from an irrelevant upper-middle-class religious hideout into a much smaller but far more nimble and authentic band of gracious fanatics who are determined to breathe a spirit that is truly holy back into its ancient lungs. My church has always been made of good stuff. Being the little boutique denomination that straddles the Protestants and the Catholics has given us an opportunity to honor both perspectives. Yet we are willing to wrestle with the nature and destiny of our individual souls and come to terms with a true meaning of personal faith. That is

---

[4] Deuteronomy 30:19.

tantamount to saying that we believe in our church and want it to be a central part of our lives.

Thankfully, we are not the purveyors of the food of spiritual infants.[5] We are not going to treat people as some do, looking to wrap their faith in shallow pretensions, cultural pabulum, or the idolatry of entitlement. A new day is dawning before our eyes, and it will be beautiful. No, it will be better than beautiful. It will be the renewal of our lives.

There has never been a better time to be spiritually authentic. Do not go to a church because it entertains you. It is not an amusement park where the rides spin around in circles like merry-go-rounds. The church is a lifelong journey. Jump on. Be connected to the faith of Jesus Christ. Discover for yourself that life is far richer when you care, when you are invested, when you are committed, when you believe, and when you are a person of faith. In other words, let yourself be transformed. And when you do, a door to a completely soul satisfying life will open.

---

[5] Cf. 1 Corinthians 3:2.

CHAPTER 1

SELL ANCESTRY

The Sell family arrived in Pennsylvania in the late 1600s. If the research of my grandfather is accurate, it seems they came from Bavaria. It was not uncommon for some immigrants to offer themselves as indentured servants for a time in order to have their way paid for. That seems to have been the case with some of my ancestors. I have often wondered just how many may have arrived that way.

In about the sixth generation of Sells in America, there was a family in Lancaster, Pennsylvania, with three children: William (born in1858), Bertha (1873), and Martin (1881). Martin seems to have had a long-term relationship with his male partner, whom, as I recall, he referred to as Dear Heart, although his name seems to have actually been Gearhart. He, Gearhart, and Bertha lived in the family home for their entire lives. When I was a young child, we would receive Christmas cards made up of photographs of Martin dressed up like Santa Claus. There was never much of a note except an expression that he and Dear Heart were doing well. I do not remember anything about Bertha.

William Drumm - or W.D., as he was always called - sought to make a life for himself beyond Lancaster. He volunteered for the U.S. Army and became a part of the Corps of Engineers. He rose to the rank of Captain and apparently acquired the nickname Cappy because of it. While in the army, he learned the trade of surveying, which was virtually the equivalent of a profession. Although he did not go to college, he had a highly marketable skill that allowed him to live wherever he wanted and to try out new experiences. Somehow, he managed to get down to West Virginia, where he was a surveyor in the coal mines.

My sister recalled the story of how he met his wife, Rose. She reported that Rosalie - or Rose, as she was called - was teaching school in a rural one-room schoolhouse, maybe in Monroe County, West Virginia. W.D. came by with a survey party and asked for a cold drink of water. She was able to accommodate him, and as they say in such stories, the rest is history. One must assume that Rose had something more than a basic high-school education. Normally, in that era, a young lady or gentleman could spend one year in a teacher's college called a Normal School and receive what was called a Standard Normal education, which was certification as an elementary teacher.

Rose's history was somewhat more accessible to me because of her West Virginia roots. While there was perhaps no notable Sell in history, we can trace Rose's history back to the Rev. John Alderson, a Church of England priest. His son, John Alderson Jr., arrived in New Jersey in 1719, indentured to a Mr. Curtis. He must not have stayed indentured for long, because when he could, he married Mr. Curtis's daughter. A later heir, George Osborne, married Mary Lohr and had nine children in tiny Gap Mills, a few miles from the county seat of Union, West

Virginia. One of those nine children, Jacob, had four children. The youngest was Rose, born in 1868.

Rose Osborne Sell was a bright, resourceful, and adventuresome young lady for her time. In the 1970s, I lived in Greenbrier County, West Virginia, the county that is contiguous to Monroe County, her childhood home. Even then, there were people in Monroe County who remembered her and spoke glowingly of her. She achieved some recognition as an artist. She was a founder of the Allied Artists of West Virginia in 1934, along with her art teacher, a long-forgotten talent known simply as Mr. Hugo. It is still an active organization. Somewhere in the archives of the state of West Virginia is a portrait of Rose Osborne Sell, executed by that teacher. At one time, I tried to barter them out of it by offering to trade some of W.D.'s vintage photographs but got nowhere.

A number of her paintings are still around. I have a couple. She was an impressionist. She was pretty good, although probably symbolic of her inner turmoil, she could make a floral painting look dark and foreboding. One of her largest paintings is located in Sunrise Art Museum in Charleston, West Virginia. It is the representation of a handsome Charleston residence. She is listed in a volume entitled *Early Art and Artists in West Virginia*. She was also a committed and vigorous supporter of the Nineteenth Amendment and women's right to vote.

When she married W.D. in 1892, they moved to Logan, West Virginia. In about 1900, they moved to Charleston. They purchased a house in a residential area called South Hills, which overlooked the Kanawha River. It was a four bedroom home. I would call it modestly middle class. They always had a well, but when indoor plumbing was possible, they constructed an addition with a bathroom and a plumbed kitchen. When they could convert from gas lighting to electric lighting, they did so. They had nine children. Three of those children died in infancy. The fourth child to be born was named Anne Kathryn Sell. She was born in 1896 and died on August 7, 1897. It is a curiosity that I did not remember that such a child had been part of that family when our daughter, Anne Kathryn Sell, was born. We named our daughter after her cousin, Anne Sell Chillingworth, and my sister, Kathryn Sell Chillingworth.

After that, the story starts to get complicated. The last child to be born to Rose and W.D., on February 12, 1908, was James Nathaniel Sell. The circumstances surrounding his birth are strange. Rose was a Southern sympathizer. As a symbol of her fervor for the "Lost Cause," she named two of her sons after Confederate war generals: Robert (E.) Lee Sell and Francis Marion Sell. When James was born on Abraham Lincoln's ninety-ninth birthday, so the story is told, she was in such a state of distress that she refused to name him. The family referred to him as "the baby" for several months. Finally, his sister Rose, a young teenager at the time, took the bull by the horns and named him James after a man one of her maternal aunts had married and Nathaniel after their grandfather, Nathaniel Sell.

In a more reasoned light, one might assume that Rose was caught in a severe postpartum depression. There is ample evidence to think that she was bipolar. There were times when she exhibited great creativity and energy. Other times, she became reclusive and less responsive. But the fact is, after nine pregnancies over a fifteen-year period, she was depleted. The sad reality is that there was never any evidence that she valued little Jimmy or showed much maternal love to him. His sister Dorothy, who was one year older, became his friend. She remained so throughout their lives.

And then there was W.D. I am not sure what to make of this man. There does not seem to be any evidence that he was an alcoholic, but something was seriously amiss. It is clear that he had a violent temper and was prone to holding grudges for extended periods of time. There is no question that he was brilliant and talented. From around 1905 onward, he became an early photographic artist. He made hundreds of images and carefully documented who was in them and where they were taken. He even did his own developing with a darkroom in his home. Additionally, he was an early researcher of family genealogy. I own copies of all of his research. Copies are also located in the New York Public Library and in certain museums and libraries of West Virginia. Third, he was a detailed surveyor and draftsman whose work was highly respected and valued. On occasion, he injected a little sarcastic humor into his work by adding cartoon-like images that reflected on some aspect of the life of the property owner. Today, this kind of professional behavior would be considered politically incorrect. The United Fuel Gas Company of West Virginia (later called Columbia Gas Transmission) acquired most of his original work, and it is part of their archives.

But oh my, he did make it hard on his family, and as far as I can tell, young Jimmy got the worst of it. Not only did Jimmy have a peculiar father, but also, it was clear that his mother limited her affection toward him. If anyone was ever seen as an unwanted child, he was. As a symbol of his rejection by his parents, William, Robert, and Francis were all given college tuitions. The two daughters, Rose and Dorothy, were each given $500 when they turned twenty-one. By contemporary standards, that was the financial equivalent of college tuition. When Jimmy came along and was ready to go to college in the late 1920s, he received nothing except two army blankets. Since W.D. was a Captain in the army and his big brother William Osborne Sell served in World War I, it is assumed that those blankets were expendable.

However, he was determined to get a college education. His timing was particularly difficult since the stock market crashed in 1929, when he was twenty-one, sending the nation into financial ruin. It was a perfectly appropriate option for him to attend the University of Cincinnati. The university was not far away from home and it was the second school in America to offer a work-study program. A student could go to school for six months and then work six months and manage to graduate in five years. He enrolled as a civil engineering student and successfully completed the course. His one source of spare cash was his winnings from playing poker and bridge for money. He would tell stories of going to the university cafeteria and getting a bowl of hot water, filling it with ketchup to make it like tomato soup, and then dropping in pickles and olives, which were hidden by the ketchup. He was a shy, timid young man, a product of classic child neglect. It was a pattern of behavior that never left him.

I think the poison that pervaded that household was not just limited to the neglect of the youngest child. In Exodus, it is said that "the sins of the father are passed on to the next generations."[6] My sense is that as soon as the children of that family were able to escape, they did. I am pretty sure I never

---

[6] Exodus 34:7.

met the daughter named Rose. William (called Osborne), Francis (Frank) and Robert (Bob) were all highly intelligent men who lived their adult lives away from their roots. Dorothy and Jim had only each other to hold on to. Dorothy lived with her husband in nearby South Charleston.

Upon graduation, Jim returned to Charleston and his family home and took a job for the Colombian Carbon Company. I do not know specifically what that work was, but it was coal based. Across the back drive from his home was a large house where Henry Watterson and Mary Simmons DePue were living. The DePues were both raised in Spencer, West Virginia, but at the time, Henry was working in Charleston, and his second youngest child, Helen Kathryn DePue, was at home. I do not know how long their courtship lasted, but on October 3, 1933, Jim and Helen were married in that Charleston home.

DePue Ancestry

Perhaps I have chosen to talk about my mother last because on some levels, I am less informed about her history. I have often wondered where the DePue family emigrated from in France. I do not know. I do know that they were always Presbyterian. A questionable three-volume book published in 1913, called *The History of West Virginia and Its People*,[7] says that they came to America as Huguenots, fleeing religious persecution. There are numerous alternative spellings for DePue and they can be found in many areas, including West Virginia, New York State and the valley of Virginia. Henry was about the sixth generation of

[7] By Thomas C. Miller.

his family in America. Somehow, his predecessors came into Roane County long before the Civil War.

Mary Simmons DePue had her roots in Scotland, but her people came to western Virginia before the Revolutionary War. My mother was accepted the Daughters of the American Revolution from tracing her lineage to a Revolutionary War officer who was tied into Mary's line. My mother was not an enthusiastic member of the DAR, but she was pleased to have that kind of genealogy. Every one of the first-born DePue sons was named Henry for generations. Even today, my family abounds in Henrys. For a long time, that first name was spelled Henri. My great-grandfather decided it was time to be more American and changed it to Henry.

One of the mythologies of the DePue family history is that they owned a considerable tract of land in northern Roane County dedicated to agriculture. At some point, natural gas was found on the property, but there was no way to develop it or export it. The legendary Godfrey L. Cabot of Boston came down through West Virginia and offered the owners one dollar per acre for their mineral rights. That seemed like a windfall since there was no way of developing those resources. Perhaps someday, a sharp historian will determine the truest story. But this we know: Cabot Fuel Company made a bonanza and the DePues made almost nothing "In the land of the bean and the cod, the Cabots speak only to Lowells and the Lowells speak only to God."[8] And no one spoke to the DePues, because they were just poor Appalachian mountain people.

---

[8] From the state song of Massachusetts written by Arthur J. Marsh (1895-1966).

My mother's father, Henry DePue, whom we called Papa Hal, somehow managed to attend college. He went to Glenville State Teacher's College in Glenville, West Virginia. He probably did the same as Rose Osborne and attended one year to be certified as a teacher. Whether or not he ever taught is unclear. He spent his time trying to make something of his life and was only moderately successful. There used to be a character in the funny papers named Major Hoople in *Our Boarding House*. Major Hoople was a potbellied blowhard who imagined himself to be of some importance, but he relied on his wife to run a boarding house for income. Henry DePue, my grandfather, reminded me of Major Hoople. Despite his limitations, my mother adored him. Throughout my childhood, I was constantly reminded of the clever political observations that allegedly poured from Papa Hal. To her, he was everything my father was not. If I were to guess, I would say she appreciated and respected her husband, but she was enraptured by her father. My father was reserved, introverted, cautious, and impossible to know. Henry was self-important, extroverted, charming, and bordering on irresponsible. His wife, Mary, whom we called Mama Mary, did most of the work while Henry preened and pontificated. His crowning achievement was his election to the West Virginia State House of Representatives from Roane County. While there, he served as Sergeant-at-Arms. I guess he was supposed to stop fistfights and prospective duels between the delegates. My notion is that it was a position given to someone who thought he ought to have a position, when no one else did.

Over a period of years, they produced six children who reached maturity. From what I can determine, the boys were holy terrors. It was clear that one did not want to get into a fight with a DePue, because he would end up fighting the whole family. Alcohol and harsh language were constants. A lack of civility was common. Even though Papa Hal went to college for a year or so, there was never any expectation that the next generation would seek professional careers. One wonders how far they got through school. I know my mother got through high school, and that achievement was looked upon as admirable. The smartest thing all of them did was marry well-grounded partners who, like Mama Mary, brought sense and sensibility to their lives. To their great credit, all of the boys served honorably in the U.S. Army in World War II.

Helen had the good sense to marry an engineer. She never worked. She did not even have a Social Security card until she was told that she could not collect her husband's Social Security if she did not have one. She was so intimidated by her brothers that she never learned to drive a car. They told her repeatedly that she would probably kill someone if she ever got behind a wheel.

HELEN AND JIM

When Helen and Jim got married, two ground rules were established. Her father had been active in Democratic politics in West Virginia before the election of Franklin D. Roosevelt. Until that point, the state was Republican. Roosevelt and the New Deal made it yellow dog[9] Democratic for the next fifty years until the Reagan revolution. My father was an Episcopalian.

---

[9] A so-called yellow-dog Democrat is someone who would vote for a yellow dog on the ballot before voting for a Republican.

His father had been the Sunday school superintendent at St. Matthew's Episcopal Church in Charleston. They took the Episcopal Church seriously. My mother took the Democratic Party very seriously. The deal was that she would become an Episcopalian and he would be a Democrat. That was how it was and nothing ever changed. She did not much care where they went to church, but she was not going to live with a Republican.

Did they have a good marriage? I know they relied on each other on many levels, and I think they were loyal to one another. They were both insecure. They were both products of family histories that were extraordinarily dysfunctional. They must have had to steel themselves against the craziness that surrounded them. That probably made my father an even more isolated man than he already was and my mother the anxious woman she was. But they were survivors and this is not damning by faint praise, I think they did the best they could. A remarkable observation about both my father's family and my mother's family is that, as far as I can tell, there was never a divorce among any of them. In an age when divorce is common, this continues to be a noteworthy feat. Part of their marital success was probably based on the tried and true Protestant ethic; however, I think a sense of total interdependence was at the foundation of it all. And all twelve of those young men and women had enough sense to know that they would be lost without their well-focused spouses.

Neither of my parents ever lived much beyond the county in which they grew up. The world was a scary place. Once, when they were retired, they took a trip to Europe. My mother said my father had nightmares about that trip for months afterward. The idea of flying on an airplane was frightening to him. Even though my father was a professional engineer, on many levels, they were Appalachian naïfs.

In 1937, the first child was born, a daughter named Helen Kathryn. They called her Kathy, but when I came along, I kept mispronouncing her name, calling her Cappy. As I said, W.D. might have been called Cappy on occasion, so the new nickname stuck. During these years, my father continued with Colombian Carbon Company. I think money was pretty tight, as the Depression was still raging (indeed, the Depression raged in West Virginia decades longer than the rest of the country) but he always had a job and they paid the bills.

MY BIRTH

On December 7, 1941, everyone's world changed. The bombing of Pearl Harbor and America's entry into World War II were pivotal moments of the twentieth century. My family's life was no different. By this time, my parents had managed to purchase a small but comfortable home on Oakmont Road in South Hills, a middle-class neighborhood. My father was thirty-four years old and employed in what was known as a critical industry: the production of coal. Because of his age and "high priority demands" of his job, he was not subject to the draft. However, three weeks after Pearl Harbor, I was conceived. If one does the arithmetic, it would seem that I was conceived on New Year's Eve, 1941. My birthdate is October 1, 1942. When I teased my parents by suggesting that I was the product of a wild New Year's Eve, they would blush, turn their heads and say nothing. They were modest, and the discussion of anything relating to reproduction was not an option. It is clear that I was conceived as an insurance policy against my father going to war.

Many years later, as my father was looking toward the end of his life, something unusual took place. He was one of the most private people I ever knew. He was not capable of talking about his hopes, fears, or dreams. He and I were alone one day, and suddenly, he said, "I wish I had gone. They could have used a good civil engineer, in World War II. I was in good shape physically. I could have done it. I wish I had gone." I felt as if I were hearing his final confession. It was the most intimate thing I ever heard from him. For forty years, he had carried within himself a shame and a sadness that he could not overcome. There were no tears or rage, there was no emotion of any kind and the last thing he probably wanted from me was absolution. The idea that his own son would tell him that he was a forgiven man was not an option. So I just smiled, patted his hand, and said nothing. As far as I can remember, it was the only intimate moment between the two of us in my life.

EARLY YEARS

Growing up in Charleston in the late 1940s and 1950s was slow, mellow and unthreatening. It was a town of about fifty-five thousand. It was so safe that when I was in late elementary school, my parents would let me walk down to the central business area alone. Because my father's office was there, I always had a place I could go if I needed to. Of course, we were in the heart of Appalachia, but it did not seem that way. The county teemed with industry. Carbide, DuPont, FMC, and other major industrial players had factories there. Carbide had a research facility there that was as sophisticated as any in the world. It was their answer to Bell Labs in New Jersey. I had many friends whose fathers were engineers, earning excellent incomes. The schools were pretty good. Several dozen boys and girls from my class at Charleston High School were accepted into highly selective colleges and universities. These days, the Gallup Poll consistently ranks Charleston as the worst place for well-being to live in America, with its sister city, Huntington, next to last. But in the 1950s, that was not so.

My first educational experience was kindergarten at South Hills Country Day School, more commonly called Mrs. Dick's. My sister had gone there five earlier. When I think back on it, I am impressed. The first thing to note was that about 10 percent of my class was Jewish, as well as one of the teachers. This would not seem like a big deal today, but in 1947 in small town, southern-oriented Charleston, it must have been seen as progressive. As it turned out, one of the most highly regarded early childhood education experts in America, Ellen May Galinsky, was one of my most beloved classmates. She has gone to have an amazing career. Two other children, Murray Abrams and Nancy Butts, and I went to school together from kindergarten all the way through college.

There was little money for us to take vacations, so my parents would put Cappy and me on a B&O Railroad train, with precise instructions to the conductor, to go visit our cousins on their dairy farm in Athens, Ohio. I was probably six or seven and she was probably eleven or twelve. Our cousins had an old World War II surplus Jeep that they used around the farm. The train conductor knew to drop us off at the Grosvenor Tower whistle stop down the road from their home and they would be there in the Jeep, waiting for us. It was fun. Cappy and the oldest DePue, Jackie, were great friends. Ginny, Ben, and Bobby were my playmates. We would gather vegetables out of their garden and then put them in a little red wagon and take them into Athens, where we sold them door-to-door. Also, we would all pile into their car and go to the Athens County Fair together.

After a few years on Oakmont Road, we bought the house across the street. It was in shambles, but my parents began the process of restoring and remodeling it. It had a generous yard and a large cherry tree and mulberry tree and was an easy walk to other children's homes.

One day, two U.S. Air Force fighter jets collided over the house. This was at the beginning of the Cold War and we were certain an atomic bomb had been dropped on us. My father grabbed us and held on while the noise, which was unlike any I have ever heard since, resounded through the neighborhood. My mother was crying that we were all going to die and I guess I must have believed her. Of course, the two pilots were killed; otherwise, the town was spared any other destruction. That was the first time I began to have the notion that my time on Earth might be somewhat brief. But there would be plenty of other warnings that I might be getting ready to, as Hamlet said, "shuffle off this mortal coil."

Around the same time, the City of Charleston was proudly opening its new airport with a big parade. To help celebrate, they invited native son, war hero, test pilot, and man with the right stuff Colonel Chuck Yeager to fly over. We found a good place to see the parade by sitting on the South Side Bridge, which crossed the Kanawha River and could look down upon it. When it came time for Yeager to fly over, he flew under us; that is, he flew under the bridge to the cheers of his admirers, the anger of the FAA, and the abject terror of my mother. It was an amazing feat, as I suspect he had only about three hundred feet of clearance and was in a fighter jet going about six hundred miles per hour.

The family across the street and a neighbor woman who occasionally kept an eye on Cappy and me both had televisions. Starting in 1951, there was one station that came on the air in mid-afternoon and shut down at 11:00 p.m. It was channel 5 (later changed to channel 3), WSAZ-NBC, in Huntington. The highlight of the week was that this station showed *I Love Lucy*. I would get myself invited over to one of those homes to watch Lucy and Desi every week. Then I would come home and describe every bit of the show to my parents. I could hardly contain my glee as I described each hilarious moment. Up to that point, they were pretty sure television was going to be just a passing fad. When they heard my constant excitement, they could not stand missing out. So the next year, they broke down and purchased a seventeen-inch (black-and-white, of course) General Electric television. Each afternoon, I would run home to watch *Howdy Doody*, the singer Kate Smith, and the first soap operas. In the summer, they carried live Cincinnati Reds baseball games. I became a fan of Joe Nuxhall and Ted Kluszewski. On several occasions, Dad and I would take a special train over to Crosley Field for the day to see a game.

Around that time, my father made a decision that, in retrospect, I would have never expected. I guess W.D. invited him to begin the process of taking over his surveying and civil engineering practice. There was a good side and a bad side to this opportunity. The good side was that W.D. had a high degree of respect in the city and my father inherited that good will from day one. Also, W.D. had extensive records of surveyed property. Therefore, it was not a difficult task for my father to take prior surveys and update them as needed. The downside was another matter. What was my father trying to do? Earn his father's approval? Overcome a lifetime of pain? I do not know and I do not know if he knew either. This mean-spirited man did not deserve to have his dutiful son at his side.

However, W.D. and my father's working relationship lasted for only a year or two. W.D. retired, my father took over the business, and it worked out well enough. No one made much money back then. In the mid-1960s, my father closed his private practice and became City Engineer for the city of Charleston. His salary hit five digits. He was making more than $10,000. You would have thought he had won the lottery.

The whole experience was hard for him. For about four or five years, he became something of a problem drinker. Was he an alcoholic? Maybe yes; maybe no. This was before the time of the general acceptance of AA and its related programs, but I do know my mother took the matter into her own hands. She had already had enough of alcohol from her father and brothers. Each night that he came home drunk, she would be merciless in her reaction. She would harass him well into the night while I sat upstairs, listening in fear and confusion. It was a devastating time. But hey, it worked. After a while, he quit and essentially never went back to drinking. Late in life, he had a little wine in the evenings, but that was about it.

In about 1950, W.D. died, and Rose moved into the penthouse at the Ruffner Hotel. Do not be impressed. It was a modest little apartment stuck on the top floor of a small hotel. She died in 1952. Their home, which was my father's childhood home, was located on Bridge Road. It had begun to fall down around them from a lack of maintenance. Over the next two years, it was trashed. The windows were broken out by neighborhood boys, and it was in a sorry state of repair. They had been successful in restoring the Oakmont Road residence, so they made the decision to purchase the family home. Despite its shabby condition and modest size, it seemed like the right thing to do. My father had to buy out his siblings' shares; the price was $500 per child, so he acquired it for $2,500. Replacing the windows was the first thing to be done, and then the roof was restored. For a month or so, the only habitable room was the kitchen where we slept on mattresses and had our meals. Actually, we managed pretty well. As they could, they cleaned up, painted and made the other rooms attractive and we had a home. That first phase took just a few months, but the whole project probably took about ten years. They made improvements as they could afford them.

DYSLEXIA AND ALLERGIES

Living in the house was a disaster for me. I now know that it was the mold, the air pollution over the city and the occasional cat that practically destroyed me. For the next ten years, I had a constantly running nose. I regularly took five or six handkerchiefs to school and brought them all home soaking wet. Antihistamines were just coming onto the market, and if I took one, it made me so groggy that all I wanted to do was sleep. I came down with asthma often enough that I had to be taken to the emergency room on a few occasions. Trying to be a successful student became difficult.

Furthermore, something else slowly began to surface; something was going on neurologically that I did not get any real clarity on for more than twenty years. My mother said, "He seems to have reversal tendencies." I was dyslexic. Dyslexia was a word that was just entering the clinical vocabulary at the time. I would finally diagnose myself in about 1975, as a thirty-three-year-old man, but looking back, I can see that the evidence was there. I would start each school year bright, chipper, and hopeful, but I would end up practically failing. My spelling was atrocious. Math and science were impossible. And perhaps most embarrassingly, I was an athletic disaster. We belonged to a local tennis and swim club and I was a poor tennis player but a good swimmer; however, swimming was not considered a *real* sport, as football and basketball were. I loved music and wished I could play an instrument, so I talked my parents into letting me take guitar lessons. I was so bad that I could not decide whether to go up or down the fret board to play higher scales. The curse of dyslexia tugged at everything I tried.

My years at Fernbank Grade School were confusing. I had a learning problem, but in addition, for reasons that I never understood, the school principal and my mother had serious issues with one another. It sounds like some line from an irritated child, but it was true. They had a confrontation about once a year. On at least one occasion, my father had to intervene on my mother's behalf when the conversation was reduced to name-calling. I was caught in the middle. It was hard. The principal would never let me do anything extracurricular if she could stop me. In fact, my teachers had to write my grades on my report card in pencil so that she could adjust them down if she wanted to! And she did on occasion.

Getting Ready To Die

Getting back to the Cold War, in about 1953, when I was in the fifth grade, something happened that was emblematic of the age. The local newspaper reported that Charleston was number fifty on the Soviet hit list in case of an all-out conflagration. The Chemical Valley, as the Chamber of Commerce proudly called it, was one of the epicenters of the Cold War, or so we were led to believe. One spring afternoon, we thought the game was over. A particularly dense thundercloud rolled across the sky and darkened the day. The principal was convinced that this was the big one. She believed that the Soviet Union must have dropped an atomic bomb somewhere and the fallout and radiation were drifting over Charleston. She got on the public address system (a newfangled addition to the school) and announced that we were under attack. We were instructed to get under our desks and cover our heads. After maybe ten minutes of cowering there in dread, she thought better of it and announced that all was well and that we could come out. But for the next fifteen years or so, I assumed that, barring any special circumstances, I would probably die in a nuclear holocaust and I expected the event to be sooner, rather than later.

Somewhere around that time, I did come close to heaven. My father had purchased perhaps his very first new car, a station wagon. I do not recall the brand, but I am sure it was new. This was at a time when American cars were poorly made and the revolution in smaller, more-efficient foreign cars had not happened yet. This car had a problem with the carburetor flooding and causing the engine to stall. It happened often. But with a new car, a little road trip seemed like a good idea. We packed up and drove over to see some of our cousins in Ohio. There were no interstate highways, just the equivalent of what we would think of today as back roads or blue highways on the road maps. We came up to a B&O railroad crossing. A train was coming, although it was fairly far down the track. There were no such things as drop-down crossing barriers, so Dad felt he had plenty of time to cross in front of the train. As he came onto the crossing the car stalled. Yikes. We were in a bad place. The way to deal with this mechanical problem was to put one's foot completely down on the accelerator, which would blow out the flooding and then start it up again. Unable to stop or even slow down from that near distance, the train was coming with its whistle screaming. Dad was sweating intensely as he tried to restart the car. Mother was screaming for us to get out of the car and run. Cappy and Mother had the doors open and were preparing to jump. Maybe I did not hear her, but I elected to roll up into a tight ball and try to get down on the floor of the car so that the metal body would provide some protection. At what seemed like the last possible second, the engine started, Mother and my sister closed the doors, and the car leapt off the crossing as the train passed. Mother was beside herself with fear and rage! She had had her wits scared out of her once again. All she could think to say was that I should have known to get out of the car, because that train would have sent me headlong down the tracks to certain death. How, may I ask, was I supposed to know that? My training for an impending disaster was to curl up on the floor, as the Civil Defense people had taught me.

Two years later, another thing happened that caused me to come face-to-face with what appeared to be my impending mortality. I was in the seventh grade at Thomas Jefferson Junior

High School. One October day, I began throwing up in school. When my mother was called, she determined that something serious was wrong. My Dad picked me up and delivered me directly to Kanawha Valley Hospital. Before the day was out, I was diagnosed with appendicitis and taken to surgery. That all went well; however, the doctor kept me there for several more days to recuperate. One afternoon, I had an uninvited guest. A rural Baptist minister was going up and down through the halls of the hospital, seeing who might be open to being saved. I guess he asked if he could talk to me. I saw no problem with that. He then began to tell me about the wages of sin and the certainty of death. I do not believe he asked me if I accepted Jesus Christ as my Lord and Savior. If he did, I am sure I had no idea what he was talking about. After all, I was an Episcopalian. We never discussed such things. But later in the day, when my parents dropped in to see me, I announced that I was going to die, but it was okay because I was saved. My mother went ballistic! She jumped on the hospital for letting this "evangelical crackpot" in my room, but the job was done. I was building a file on impending death in my head and it would continue to grow for a number of years into the future.

Despite my educational drawbacks, I had other abilities that I did not know what to make of. While I struggled to learn visually, I was over the top with aural learning. I developed a strong vocabulary, and I could remember many things precisely. I could remember whole conversations. I could listen to a popular song once or twice and have it memorized. To this day, I am pretty good at answering the questions on the TV show, *Jeopardy,* and working challenging crossword puzzles.

Most of these memoirs are the present-day remnants of that overactive memory.

But I could not do most of my schoolwork. By about my junior year in high school, I was telling myself two things at the same time: "I am not too smart" and "I surprise myself with what I know." Rather than do my homework, I immersed myself in other learning. Because my mother never went to college, she took it upon herself to be self-educated. She subscribed to classical records from the Columbia classical records club, took classes in a series called the Great Books at the Charleston Library, and subscribed to publications like the *Saturday Review, Harpers*, and the *Atlantic*. In elementary school, my friends and I purchased Classics comic books and traded them around. These were comic books that recounted classic novels. I became conversant about many great books years before Cliff's Notes came along. Do not misunderstand: I certainly could read. I was slow, but I was insatiable. I devoured books. By high school, I became a fan of both twentieth century American fiction and modern American history. I read Hemingway, Faulkner, Sinclair Lewis, F. Scott Fitzgerald, and, of course, J.D. Salinger and Jack Kerouac, as well as many other authors of both fiction and nonfiction. I acquired a copy of Bartlett's *Familiar Quotations* and without trying to, I was able to remember sections of speeches by great orators, such as Winston Churchill and F.D.R., as well as a whole panoply of obscure literary minutia. I would have never imagined that a day would come when I could put this knowledge to good use! But as a preacher, I pulled it out of my memory on practically a weekly basis. All the while, my grades were abominable and my confidence as a student tanked.

One of the principal joys of my social life was to gather with a small group of friends at the home of Martha Neff. Martha had a family room that, we were assured, was soundproof. This was the era of the folk music revival. Together, we had stacks of thirty-three r.p.m. albums by popular folk singers, such as the Kingston Trio and Harry Belafonte, and lesser knowns, such as the Weavers, Leadbelly, Odetta, the Clancy Brothers, and Josh White (Peter, Paul and Mary did not come along until 1962). None of us could play a musical instrument, so we would sing along with the records in happy harmony. Oh, the innocence of it all. And what fun!

Because I was prevented from achieving in elementary school and because my neurological and physical heath became more problematic as I got older, the Boy Scouts was one of the two programs that rescued me. I belonged to a well-run troop hosted by the local Presbyterian church. The scout master, James R. Thomas, was a young man of great integrity who gave me a fair chance to succeed. Rising through the ranks of scouting to become an Eagle was a singular success of my youth. I would spend my summers attending camps. For a few years, I went to a private camp in Virginia called Wallawhatoola. My father was doing well at the time, so my parents could afford to spring for it. Later, I went to Boy Scout camps and the diocesan church camp. I was glad to get away from home and not be burdened by both the allergies and various little demons that I lived with in that house.

Because my sister was five years older, she and I practically lived separate lives. But, around that time, she did do me two wonderful favors. Believe it or not, Charleston High School had fraternities and sororities. There was no way I was going to get into one; I did not have the social, athletic, or academic skills. Even though she was already in college, she still had the contacts to break the ice and I was invited to join one. In like manner, she had a friend a little older than she was who had come back to Charleston High School as the teacher responsible for the school paper, *The Bookstrap*. My sister talked to her before the start of high school and I was invited to be on the paper. Participating in the school paper was the second lifesaver for me. The teacher, Ann Garrity, more than took pity on me. She treated me with respect and dignity. She did not seem to know much about my health and reversal tendencies, but she bent over backward to care about me, despite the fact that I was not a prized pupil.

Once my father became a self-employed civil engineer, he found that he needed part-time help. For most of his career, he offered jobs to boys who were students at Morris Harvey College.[10] It was a good part-time job. He would work in the office in the mornings and then go on surveying field trips in the afternoons, using these college students as his crew. Of course, if the weather was cold or wet, the boys would have the afternoon off and he would continue working in his office. When I was thirteen, he decided that he could kill two birds with one stone. In the summers, he would use me and pay me well. Then, during the school year, he would rely on the Morris Harvey boys. He did this so that he could help me have money for college while he treated me as a business expense. I liked working for my father. I could see that he was a good man who cared deeply for me, despite his inability to express his feelings. This system continued through some of my undergraduate

---

[10] Later, the school was renamed the University of Charleston.

college years, so I can say that with the exception of a few short breaks in my history, I worked steadily from about 1955 until my final retirement in 2013.

I had two other jobs during that time. For a while, I worked at a Kroger grocery store, checking people out. I guess I did well enough. Those old cash registers were certainly not designed for people with dyslexia, but I managed. Also, one summer, I was an intern at an antipoverty program of President Kennedy's New Frontier, called Action for Appalachian Youth. That training ended up giving me some excellent skills in relating to mountain people which I was able to use, until I left West Virginia in 1980.

Frankly, it is a little amazing that I survived those years. Some of my peers did not. Between about 1958 and 1965, about ten boys and girls I knew were killed in violent car wrecks. I could have been one of them but was spared. As I said, I was expecting an early death. The dice seemed to be loaded against me. It was just a matter of time. I knew I was going to die young, but I was betting on the atomic bomb, not some clunky used car.

However, the cars did their best to fulfill my deeply fatalistic beliefs. When I was sixteen, I bought a 1952 Nash Rambler for $200 with my Kroger money. That was the car in which I learned to drive. Two years later, I bought another, a 1952 Ford, also for $200. One night, I went to a Charleston High School basketball game and I agreed to pick up several friends and drive them to the game. It was a cold night. On the way home, I had a flat tire, the battery went dead, the radiator boiled over, and I ran out of gas. When I arrived home around eleven o'clock, my parents were certain that I was lying about my misadventures, but the story I told them was the truth. There was no way I could have contacted them to let them know of my distress.

I cannot say that I was popular. I was well-known but rather marginalized when it came to the most popular students. I dated a couple of girls in high school, but always felt awkward and unsure.

Two boys ended up being the most important and the longest lasting friends I had. I first met them both in the seventh grade. As a sophomore in high school, Frank G. Kirkpatrick began reading philosophy and religion. One day, he announced that he was reading *I and Thou* by the German Jewish philosopher Martin Buber. He suggested I read it. It was, without a doubt, the most confusing piece of literature I had ever seen in my life up to that point, yet I was impressed that he was reading it. Years later, I wondered whether he really understood it as a sixteen year old. I do not know. However, he did decide that he wanted to study religion in college as an academic pursuit and that opened for me the possibility of a new subject that I had never considered before. Frank went on to earn a Ph.D. in religion from Brown University; and he has written nine books and spent his career in the religion department at Trinity College in Hartford, Connecticut. His latest book, *The Mystery and Agency of God: Divine Being and Action in the World*[11] is brilliant. My guess is that Frank did fully comprehend Buber when he was sixteen! He was smart enough. At the close of my career, I accepted a position as the Interim Rector of Trinity-on-the-Green, New Haven, Connecticut. Among my reasons

---

[11] Fortress Press: Minneapolis(2014)

for accepting this call was because Frank and his wife, Liz, were in the area.

Chet Shuman was like Frank only in that both of them were brilliant. The oldest of four boys with a father who encouraged his engineering and scientific explorations, Chet was a math and science whiz. However, there was nothing nerdy about him. He would sneak out in the middle of the night with the best of us to explore the town. Smoking cigarettes and drinking beer (3.2 "near beer," thank you very much) were both common. Chet did his part. But when he scored an 800 on advanced mathematics and excelled on the other College Board tests, he was accepted to Harvard and began a life that was way outside of my academic orbit. However, we stayed close through college and, like Frank, he remains one of my best friends today. Chet became the owner of a successful software business in Boston. It provided computer services to architects in every state of the union. Today, an occasional delight is an invitation to the Shuman home on Westport Island in Maine, where Chet and his wife, Evelyn, spend their summers.

By this time, I should be sharing a little background about my life in the church. As I said earlier, I was always an Episcopalian. I was baptized at St. Matthew's Church in South Hills, Charleston. W.D. and Rose were my godparents. However, I never attended there (except for Cub Scouts and endless ballroom-dancing classes!). From as early as I can remember, my family attended the downtown church, St. John's. After World War II, everybody either went to church or said they did. I did not know a single child who was not a part of a congregation of one kind or another. As might be consistent with other things I have said, I had no idea what

my parents' religious life consisted of. Were they persons of
faith? Did they just go for cultural reasons? We never talked
about religion. The prevailing attitude of the era was that one
did not discuss one's faith. Like money and sex, faith was seen
as too personal and outside the realm of polite conversation.
Anything too self-revealing was impossible for my father to
cope with. He preferred to hide behind a wall of silence. On
the other hand, my mother, the extrovert, was happy to get
up, get dressed, go to church, and visit with other members of
the congregation. In her later years, they would skip worship
altogether and arrive immediately afterward for the coffee hour,
the social opportunity she loved. Religion never seemed to be
her main interest. But the Episcopal Church was seen as the
upper-middle-class denomination in those days, and she liked
that a lot.

My sister and I attended dutifully. We had no choice. From
about age thirteen all the way into college, I often served as
an acolyte or altar boy. At least it gave me something to do.
For the most part, I did not have a positive attitude toward the
church and worship. Most of the ethos of the congregation was
one of benign indifference. People attended because the wider
culture expected it, but nothing spiritually transformative ever
seemed to happen. Most of the preachers spoke elliptically
without ever using concrete terms or illustrations. The image
of a significant preacher was a man (yes, always a man) who
looked and sounded somewhat like a professor and seemed
serious from the pulpit. It was not the message that needed to
be stimulating; style points were what counted. A clergyman
would mount the pulpit. The lights would go down in the
congregation; a spotlight glowed in a heavenly way on him,

and the congregation members felt as if they were in touch with something sacred. I remember a best-selling book at the time called *How to Be a Bishop Without Being Religious* by Charles M. Smith[12]. It was intended to be funny, and it was! The sum and substance of the book was that if a cleric wanted to be a bishop, he should look religious but not too religious, smile benevolently but never laugh, and act smart but never outshine the members of the church. The sad truth was that it was a pragmatic guide to being elected a bishop!

Finally, in about 1958, a young assistant rector named Bill Pregnall came to St. John's. Bill was well-educated, well-read, broad-minded, and interested in young adults and youth. He could be clever and humorous in his preaching. He was also articulate, transparent, and honest. I was enamored and enthralled. He was the most appealing clergyperson I had ever seen or heard. I cannot say that I became a believer in the claims of Jesus Christ through Bill's mentoring, but I did have a role model of a person in the ordained ministry who seemed to be imbued with openness and intelligence. Somewhere along the line, I began to toy with the notion that if I could be in the same mold as Bill Pregnall, I could contemplate the ministry as a profession.

A whole lot else was going on in the 1950s and '60s that would define me forever. One October day, as a twelve-year-old in 1954, I walked home from school only to be met by my mother at the corner where our driveway met the street. She was in tears. She said, "Oh Jimmy, something terrible has happened today." My gosh, I thought someone, such as my father or sister, must have died! She went on to say, "The

---

[12] Pocket Books, a division of Simon and Schuster: New York (1965).

Supreme Court has decided that from now on, you will have to go to school with colored children." And then she cried some more. But here is the rest of the story. Six months later, she had completely changed her attitude. Somehow, she knew that this new reality was the right thing. I do not know what my father thought. As usual, he kept his own counsel. But my mother became a proponent for the civil rights of African Americans. That is not to say she became a public activist, but her liberal heart was there.

SHOCK AND AWE

Brown v. the Board of Education of Topeka, Kansas, opened the door to decades of transforming events in my life and in almost all of them, I found myself responding like my mother. First, I felt shock that such an unexpected and momentous thing was happening. After I digested the reality, there was awe that the forward march of human history was continuing right in the midst of my life. The most significant transformation of the second millennium of the Common Era was the liberation of individuals. From the Magna Carta in the thirteenth entury until my lifetime, the ragged but inexorable journey of human freedom has been unabated. I have been awed by this ongoing story. I saw freedom as a good thing and my life would be better and more democratic because of it.

Something else happened in the late 1950s: John F. Kennedy, the charismatic young senator from the state of Massachusetts, began to run for President of the United States. He was my mother's Democratic dream. When it became clear that this Irish Catholic candidate needed to win in the West Virginia primary because that state had a small percentage of Roman

Catholics, she jumped in and became a committed volunteer. How I wish I had had a camera on one particular occasion. As I said earlier, she did not drive. One night, around ten o'clock, my dad and I got a call from her, asking us to pick her up in front of the Daniel Boone Hotel, the Kennedy campaign headquarters where she was helping out. We drove down there and sitting on the front steps, chatting, were my mother and Bobby Kennedy, JFK's campaign manager. It is an image that I continue to carry in my mind to this day.

I have long since become realistic about John F. Kennedy. The old joke was that "Papa Joe" Kennedy did not buy West Virginia in the primary election; he just rented it for the day. There were many sides to his personality. I have read many biographies written about him and his family. In many ways, I have come to admire him more as I grow older. I think politicians are just people; they have personal strengths and weaknesses. If they can stand above their personal faults, I will be appreciative of their defining professional character. This I know. Up to that point, there had never been anyone in public life who gave me more hope and more of a sense that it was wonderful to be an American. When he said in his inaugural address, "Ask not, my fellow citizens, what your country can do for you. Ask what you can do for your country,"[13] I heard that call and I yearned to respond. Kennedy made me want to be a patriot. The day he was assassinated, the hope of

---

[13] Chris Matthews, in his engaging book *John F. Kennedy, Elusive Hero* (2012), reports that the genesis of this quote is from the old headmaster of Choate School in Wallingford, Connecticut, George St. John, who "once or twice a year" encouraged his students to "ask not what Choate can give…" Some sixty years later, my son, Andrew, had the privilege of attending Choate and learning from St. John's successors.

politics was snuffed out for me. I was thankful that Lyndon B. Johnson pushed forward the agenda of the New Frontier which he renamed the Great Society. But Johnson was coarse, overly manipulative, and abrasive. Furthermore, he could not resist what seemed, to me, to be the southern politician's yearning for war. The Vietnam War was the beginning of the end of anything we knew that felt like "one nation, indivisible." From the Gulf of Tonkin Resolution to today, America has continued to grow more divided.

COLLEGE

It was clear that I was not going to set the academic world on fire. My high school grades were abominable. Perhaps today someone would have diagnosed my dyslexia and I would have been given special remediation. Maybe modern medications could have relieved my constant rhinorrhea and other health issues. That was not how things were done back then. I think it was a good thing that I was forced to compete against the other students academically. I usually lost, but I always kept trying. Had I been put on a special track, I would have been embarrassed and depressed. The struggle was good for me. Never giving up or quitting became my method of operating since I rarely achieved success easily.

It was a state law that if one graduated from a West Virginia high school, West Virginia University had to accept him or her. They did not need to keep you, but they had to give you a shot. So in the fall of 1960, I took off for Morgantown and West Virginia University. In fact, I had never even thought about going anywhere else. That was where my sister went and I was comfortable following in her footsteps. My world was pretty circumscribed by the borders of the state of West Virginia. How I arrived at the choice of a major was rather pathetic, but it all worked out in the end. The only subject I ever got an A in while I was in high school was American history, so I declared my major in history and hoped for the best. I had no career goals. I was not a prized student, but each semester, my grades improved. Along the way, I earned minors in English and political science. A smattering of philosophy and French were thrown in as well. So by the time I was a senior, I had achieved a good liberal arts education. I had some fabulous professors. I still tell teenagers that a fine education can be acquired at almost any American college or university. All one has to do is ask around to find out who the excellent professors are and they are there awaiting the students.

In the fall of 1960, West Virginia University had about six thousand students. By the time I left, the student body had more than doubled in population. Today, it has five times more students than it did when I was there. I was at the end of "silent generation." We were the ones who followed the "greatest generation." Right behind me, the "baby boomers" swarmed into college. When I arrived in college, the social life was made up of fraternities and sororities; there was no other option. In other words, if a male student had not been part of a fraternity, it would have been a barren existence. Again, I was not exactly the center of anyone's social circle, so it was not easy for me to be invited to join a fraternity. However, I did get to join the one that I wanted the most and had a manageable social life. Even though I loved a good party, I was pretty ambivalent about fraternity life. That fraternity's corporate life was similar to the film *Animal House*. Toga parties really were an annual affair.

Social probation was a constant due to the drunken parties. I lived in the fraternity house for three years, and fortunately, a distant cousin of mine, Bob Brown, and I roomed together for two of those years. I was always in search of stable people to help me stay focused and he filled the bill admirably. I suspect that if I had come along five years later, I would not have joined any fraternity. I was ahead of the curve that produced the hippies and radical left politics. The silent generation did the safe thing. We conformed. Those behind me seized power.

I probably spent more time worrying about the upcoming fraternity party and whom I was going to take to it than whether I could make an A on a test. Frankly, I think I was so profoundly lonely that trying to connect with the right girl was like trying to connect with my soul. I yearned to be loved and I yearned to have a life that was not fraught with such ambiguity.

In February 1963, Craig Ramey, a fraternity brother, told me that his girlfriend, Pat, had just met a girl who had transferred to WVU for the start of the second semester of the year. Both Craig and his girlfriend were psychology students, so when they announced to me that they thought this was the girl I was going to marry, I paid attention. To think that someone thought there might be a girl out there just for me filled my heart with hope and longing.

CHAPTER 2

ELLEN

Ellen Dorothy Major came from a family that bore fewer of the splotches that my family possessed. Her parents had come from somewhat modest circumstances, but they had successful lives and were productive people. Both of them were college graduates. Ellen's mother, Marjorie McElrath Major, grew up in the rural western Kentucky town of Murray. She leaped through school and began college at age sixteen. Although she was a Methodist, she attended Brenau College, a historically Baptist women's college in Gainesville, Georgia. Upon graduating, she became the first consumer affairs director for Procter and Gamble in Cincinnati. Her job was to take teams of young ladies around the country, where they went door-to-door in residential neighborhoods. These young ladies would ask housewives to try new products and review them for P&G. It does not sound like much today, but it was the beginning of what became a huge arm of Procter and Gamble's corporate program.

Her father, William Samuel Major, grew up in the small town of Roebling, New Jersey, which was the company town for Roebling Industries, a producer of steel rope cables and the builder of the Brooklyn Bridge. His father, Samuel Major, was the postmaster of the town and ran the local general store.

The public school probably only went through about the eighth grade. A local benefactor made it possible for him to attend Bordentown Military Academy, which is now out of business, for high school. Ellen likes to recount the stories her father told of taking the train from Roebling to Bordentown. From there, he attended nearby Lehigh University, where he majored in engineering. He was bright, personable, and, influenced by that military school regimen, always neatly dressed. He had worked for corporations in Cincinnati and Philadelphia. In Cincinnati, he met Marjorie, whom everyone called Mac, and married her. At the time we met, he worked for Dravo Corporation, a Wilmington, Delaware-based shipbuilding firm that also had a coal dust abatement division in Pittsburgh. Ellen's older brother, Robert Lear Major, was born in 1937. After graduating from Mt. Lebanon High School, Bob went to Princeton. When Ellen and I met, he had just graduated and was working on a Master's degree in mineral economics at Penn State University. From there, he joined the second class of Peace Corps volunteers in the era of its founding director, R. Sargent Shriver. He spent two years in Cyprus, engaged in a geological survey.

Ellen was born in 1942 in Bryn Mawr, Pennsylvania, but grew up in Mt. Lebanon. She attended Mt. Lebanon High School, where she graduated in 1960. She was editor of the yearbook and was broadly active in the life of the school. I think her religious life was not much different from mine, except she was a Methodist. Methodists probably think Episcopalians are a little loose when it comes to proper decorum. Methodists are far more imbued with classic American Protestantism than the Episcopalians are.

She was accepted into Methodist-based Randolph-Macon Women's College in Lynchburg, Virginia,[14] and began her academic life there. In one of the shrewdest moves of her life, she elected to major in Latin. Randolph-Macon had a well-regarded Latin program. It turned out that every time she sought a job, she was offered a position teaching Latin or English. Who would have ever guessed? The options were limited for young women back then. Teaching, nursing, or secretarial work were the principal career choices at that time. In fact, Ellen has a great analytical mind and could have done many other things. I think she would have been a terrific Certified Public Accountant or financial adviser, had she been given the opportunity to explore other alternatives.

After two years at Randolph-Macon, she had had enough. The school was small. It was all girls. The town was isolated. So in the fall of 1962, she announced to her parents that she was not going back. I am sure they were distressed. Having been an executive, her mother was strong-willed and insisted on guiding the decisions for the family. When Ellen exerted this independence, it was outside of the family norms and threw everyone for a loop, but she did it. So much for a member of the silent generation being a conformist! Instead, she went to work in the Christmas shop at Gimbels department store. It was not long before she realized that she wanted to return to college. West Virginia University was just about seventy-five miles away from her home and had a small Latin program. (How small? One semester, she was the only major.) She applied for the second semester of her third year and, of course, was readily accepted.

---

[14] Now called simply Randolph College.

Within her first few weeks there, we were fixed up. The problem was that no one had told her that I was the man of her dreams. Or if anyone had, she was not nearly as thrilled by this information as I was. I was mostly interested in having a girlfriend. She was there, heaven forbid, to get an education. While I chased her, she chased her classes. In fact, she was so highly regarded that after a year, she was appointed the editor-in-chief of the West Virginia University yearbook, the *Monticola*. It was a big job with great demands. She got paid based on the sales of the yearbook and ended up doing well enough financially to buy herself a used white Ford convertible. Because she had skipped a semester and had to limit her classes when she was editor, she ended up graduating in 1965, the year after I did.

WHAT NOW?

Toward the end of my senior year, I had no idea what to do. My bachelor's degree in American history was not worthless to me, but no one was clamoring to hire me. Besides, I was not interested in leaving Morgantown, so I enrolled in law school. I got into law school by the same hook I had used to get into undergraduate school. It was a state law that if you graduated from West Virginia University, the law school had to accept you. Again, they did not have to keep you, but they had to give you a shot.

I was completely unprepared for law school. I did not understand the concepts. I had no aspirations to be a lawyer. I was desperately confused and depressed. I struggled to get through and had visions of returning to Charleston and being a mediocre lawyer. It was a bad time in my life. I went through a prolonged period of panic attacks that were so grim that I was fearful for my life. The one glimmer of joy I had was the summer between my first and second years, when I researched land titles for the United Fuel Gas Company. I spent most of that summer in beautiful Moorefield, West Virginia. In the evenings, I would play Scrabble with law school classmate (He later became the Dean of the WVU Law School) John Fisher and his wife, Susan, while we listened to the sound track from *The Sound of Music* over and over again. I am no psychologist, so I do not know if calling my episodes panic attacks is the most accurate diagnosis, but I lived with a kind of existential dread much of the time. I was afraid I might actually be dying. All those little confrontations with death continued to crop up and kept filling my head.

On top of that, Ellen announced that she had been hired to teach Latin at Louisville Collegiate School, a girl's private day school in Kentucky and so off she went to explore new vistas. I was dazed and confused. Halfway through my second year of law school, I had had enough. I did not know what I was going to do, but I was not going to be a lawyer. I concocted a plan; it was half-baked at best, but what else was new? By that time, the Vietnam War was raging, and I had friends getting killed in Southeast Asia. There was still a Selective Service, and I did not want to be drafted. Let me be perfectly clear: despite my raging anxieties, I did not have a death wish. Dying in a rice paddy in Southeast Asia for a war that seemed unnecessary was nothing I wanted to have happen. As it turned out, my draft number was 359 out of a possible 365. I would never be drafted with a number like that, but there was no way for me to know it at that time.

With little prior consideration, I decided I would go to seminary. I was tired of being supported by my parents. I figured that if I went to seminary, I could get a full-ride scholarship and avoid the draft. But I had no intention of getting ordained. I wanted to get a Master's degree in a field that had a social bent to it. I would then try to get a job in the federal government in one of several areas. Maybe I could start off in the Job Corps, the Peace Corps, or VISTA (Volunteers in Service to America) and end up in an administrative position. All of those were Great Society programs that I felt some passion for. I was still living in the glow of "Ask not, my fellow citizens…"

Applying for seminary and candidacy for ordination was a far simpler process in 1966 than it is today. I trotted myself down to Charleston and had a meeting with the bishop, the Rt. Rev.[15] Wilburn C. Campbell. I told him I was religious and a person of faith, even though none of that was true. He seemed satisfied enough and suggested that I apply to the Episcopal seminaries in Cambridge, Massachusetts, and Alexandria, Virginia. I did, and, much to my amazement, I was accepted by both. When Virginia Theological Seminary (VTS) offered me a complete financial package that could be granted to anyone the Bishop of West Virginia elected, the decision was made.

In the fall of 1966, I began my theological education at VTS. There are no words to adequately describe how much I loved being there. When I walked onto the campus, it was the first time I had ever been somewhere where no one knew me. People did not know my history with its complications, uncertainties,

---

[15] Rt. is the abbreviation for Right. The proper title of an Episcopalian bishop is the Right Reverend. Right is a fifteenth century English word defined as "most" or "very".

and ambiguities. All they knew was what they saw and they seemed to accept me at face value. This experience produced a kind of personal liberation I had never known. To say that I was free to be anyone I wanted to be was not quite correct, but I was free to explore and discover the values I could claim as true for myself. I had taken the train from Charleston and arrived with just two suitcases of clothes; no books or dormitory necessities. Maybe I thought I was not going to last long, so there was no point in getting too settled in. I was assigned to Madison Hall, one of the dorms, and was surrounded by people who became some of my best and longest lasting friends. Ed Covert and Bob Hardman were in my wedding. There were many others whom I still stay connected to. Ed, Bob, Peter Kreitler, Len Freeman and Leslie Smith have been lifelong fellow journeyers. Even though we are physically far removed from one another at times, our professional and personal paths have intersected over and over again.

The class work was both interesting and accessible. By that time, I had learned a technique for studying that was perfect for me. I would take copious notes in my lecture classes. Then I would go over to the "preaching laboratory," a barren basement room in of one of the classroom buildings, to dictate my notes onto their reel-to-reel tape recorders. I would listen to them three or four times and have them down cold. I gained what I could from the books, but it was in the lectures and dialogue with my classmates that I really garnered information. Again, I still did not know that I was dyslexic, but I had figured out how I learned best through my years of trial and error. Thus, from the start, I made good grades and felt pleased with myself. I was doing so well that I was asked to tutor some of my struggling classmates and I was thrilled to do so.

THIS MUST BE REAL

One day, something happened that was one of the cornerstone events of my life. It was mid-October and I decided to take an afternoon nap. Upon falling asleep, I had the most galvanizing dream I have ever had. Call it a spiritual experience, such as St. Paul's Damascus Road moment or John Wesley's being 'strangely warmed". Whatever it was, I can only call it a singular event that pivoted me from past tense to future tense.

Here is the dream. I was walking through a wooded area with the young man who lived across from me in the dorm. His name was, believe it or not, J.C. Emerson (James Carson, not Jesus Christ). As we walked along, we came upon a glen. In the glen was a pool table (not surprising since I spent many of my high school afternoons in the Strand Pool Hall in Charleston). By the pool table was the man who was in charge of it. He said to me, "Would you like to shoot pool?" I said yes. He then racked up the balls into a traditional triangle. From above my line of vision, the cue ball came down onto the table, tethered to an elastic cord. It kind of plopped down and settled there. As I drew the cue back to break the balls and started forward, the cue ball was lifted off the table by the elastic cord. Thus, my forward motion with the cue resulted in nothing but disturbed air. The man behind the table then said, "I am going to give you one more chance." Once again, the cue ball drifted down upon the table attached to the elastic cord. This time, I drew back and slammed the cue into the cue ball as hard as I could. In

something that can only happen in a dream, all fifteen balls—
plunk, plunk, plunk—dropped into the various pockets.

Then J.C. and I continued on our walk. I came upon a
television set. It was turned on and the voice on the television
said to me, "This life is presented to you in living green. This
is the most living thing you have ever seen." And from out of
the television came a hand holding a green potted plant.

Then I woke up. During that time, I was still experiencing
panic attacks, and I thought I must be having yet another
warning that I was going to die. Nothing else could explain
the dream to me, because it was so personal, symbolic and
evocative. I walked next door to the room of Tad deBordenave.
Tad was someone that I had rarely encountered before: a real,
live, faith-filled Christian. I told him the dream and asked him
what he thought it meant. I was befuddled. Tad did not know
what my hidden agenda for seminary was. He assumed that I
was there for the same reason he was: to prepare myself for
ordination to the Episcopal priesthood. Then he said, "Has God
specifically called you to the ministry, Jim?"

"Well, no," I said in all honesty.

"He has now!" Tad said.

I believed it, but I really could not believe it.

Everything I had ever explored for my life and every
venture I had considered had been like taking a shot with a
cue ball and whiffing the whole experience. In this dream, I
had felt connected to something authentic for the first time.
There was nothing in my makeup or history that would have
added up to my going into the ministry. And yet, here it was:
God's big surprise. To this day, I have never known anyone
else who decided to go to seminary and then got called by God.

Everyone else does it the other way around. God calls a person, and he or she responds. Also, to this day, I have never been surer of anything than the clarity of that moment. Much to my continuing amazement, I am living the life I am supposed to be living and trying to be humble about it. Because of it, I am filled with a kind of inner joy that I never thought would be mine. Since that moment, I have always tried to slam that cue ball with as much driving force as I could muster. I sought to put as much energy as possible into my tasks. There would be good times interwoven with difficulties. Through it all, I knew I was called and I was grateful to be able to honor that call. My years of panic attacks ended and I never suffered from them again.

The three years of seminary were a whole new ball game for me. Suddenly, my life was not about waiting to die. Now I wanted to get into the process of learning to live. I did not know much about the art of living. Of course, I loved people and I loved learning. I loved the sweetness of life. But I was as walled off from my own soul as a rural Appalachian who does not know that a big, beautiful world is out there waiting to be explored. I wanted to know if God really existed and whether traditional religion had anything to offer humanity. I wanted to understand the history and claims of the Christian church. I wanted to slip underneath those claims and see if they were mere "opium of the people"[16] or attached to some underlying, saving reality.

---

[16] This quote is attributed to Karl Marx. The full quote is as follows: "Religion is the sigh of the oppressed creature, the heart of a heartless world, just as it is the spirit of a spiritless situation. It is the opium of the people" (*Critique of Hegel's Philosophy of Right*, 1844).

Therefore, my theological education had to begin at the most elementary level. A modern theological student would not be able to grasp how unprepared I was for seminary. I had hardly ever read the Bible. When it was read in church, I would slip into a kind of neutral trance. Episcopalians simply did not get into the fine details of Christianity. Reading the Bible was for others. Many of us were cultural Christians. We would have never wanted to be seen even holding a Bible in our hands much less reading it. I was so poorly prepared that I actually thought that the Joseph of the Hebrew scripture, best known for his coat of many colors, was the earthly father of Jesus, of Mary and Joseph fame. Because I was a historian, I had a fairly clear understanding of European history and its interwoven religious connections. I knew of the Reformation on both the European continent and in England. That was about it. But for the first time in my life, I was an eager learner in a prescribed, goal-oriented way. I still do not think that I was a person of faith. The jury was still out. There was too much about religion that I found dishonest, spiritually demeaning, and foolish, but I was willing to bend over backward to have my doubts resolved.

As I said, I loved being there. Not only did I fit in, I discovered that I was something of a leader and felt as if I could make something of myself in the ministry. This is not to say that I aspired to lofty goals. The notion of being a bishop, for example, never appealed me. Through it all, I did begin to believe that I could live a life of some personal self-worth. Maybe I could empathize with some people who were encountering some of the internal trials and doubts that had raged in me. That meant everything to me.

Making Discoveries

The two summers in my seminary career were of particular interest. In the summer of 1967, I lived in New York City. Every seminary student was required to take something called Clinical Pastoral Education (CPE) at a general hospital, mental hospital, or prison. I applied for and was accepted into the program at St. Luke's Hospital on the Upper West Side, across from Columbia University. At the same time, I lived about a hundred blocks south in the Chelsea neighborhood, at the General Theological Seminary. The hospital experience was tame. I am told that in some programs, the supervisor would engage in a rather extensive evaluation of the student's psychological predispositions for ordination. The process could get threatening. St. Luke's, we had little of that. A lot of the pastoral ministry training at that time operated on psychological therapy models. I did not object to that. I learned a lot I would eventually need to know. In fact, in just seven or eight years' time, I was able to work as a part-time mental health counselor and could carry my weight pretty well. Mostly, the training revolved around our bedside manner and ability to listen with sensitivity. During that summer, there were riots all around the country and many were not far from where I was living. I could go up onto the roof of my apartment building and see the smoke rising from the torching of Newark. I would get off the subway in the morning at 125th Street, known as the main street of Harlem, and the litter of the prior night's angry mobs filled the streets.

Living on the edge of Greenwich Village was a whole other experience. I had known of gay people in college and certainly had some of them closeted away in my fraternity. What had been a trickle of gay awareness became a flood in Greenwich Village. Walking down Christopher Street in the late 1960s, one encountered every kind of sexual orientation and lifestyle imaginable. The initial shock of experiencing people who were substantially different from me was soon transformed into a kind of awe. I do not think that I had ever met a gay person living out his or her orientation in a public way. While it would be a few more years before I could claim any gay persons as friends, that door began to open for me. I made a personal decision at that time that I would no longer tell gay jokes. The old frat house bashing had never been funny in the first place and now I knew it. This was two years before the famous Stonewall Grill riots in Greenwich Village that began the public transformation of gay culture, but it was there in open and honest ways even then.

The following summer, the summer of 1968, was the antithesis of my New York experience. In those days, the traditional second summer was a time of living in a parish in your home diocese. I was assigned to St. Luke's Church, Welch, which is in the heart of the extremely depressed coal mining area of West Virginia, in McDowell County. I had the specific task of conducting weeklong Vacation Bible Schools for children in five Episcopal congregations. These churches were in the towns of Welch, War, Avondale, Keystone, and Mullins. I could write a whole book on that experience alone. Each of these communities was abjectly poor and culturally distressed. St. Paul's Church in Avondale was a particular case in point. I have no idea how the Episcopal Church ended up being the only Christian congregation in the hollow, but there we were! Of course, the church was not some Gothic gem. It was a threadbare little whitewashed cinderblock building with two outhouses in the back. It had Prayer Books, a little electric organ, and hymnals with shaped notes. Shaping notes began in the early eighteenth century for people who could not read music in the traditional sense. Each of the basic notes on the eight note scale was in a different shape. It was a technique that continued to be used in rural Appalachia well into the late twentieth century. I had learned some skills in relating to Appalachian people when I spent the summer working for Action for Appalachian Youth five or six years earlier. That training held me in good stead.

Believe it or not, even in that poverty-stricken world, there were differences in social status. The dividing lines were precisely defined by the physical elevation of the different homes in the hollow. The residents had come up with names to identify themselves. At the bottom of the hollow were the people who were known as the "goods". The goods were often the Episcopalians. Many of them had jobs in the mines and were seen as the leaders of the community. They kept their tiny homes neat and their yards trimmed. No one would ever have said they were well-off, but for them, life was pretty good.

Driving up the country road, one encountered the get-alongs". As the name suggests, these people managed to get along. Perhaps they had welfare checks, black lung payments, or some form of Social Security, but their living was pretty much hand to mouth. I would not care to characterize them too specifically, because it would be demeaning to have them perceived as cartoonish people out of the comic strips. I am not sure why, but I seemed to gravitate to the get-alongs. They held on to life with a vague hope that I admired. I remember going to their homes. One couple and I would sit on their front porch, overlooking the hillside. She played the guitar left-handed (which is upside down and backward – one smart woman!) and the three of us would sing mournful country ballads ("I used to be a big man in Detroit City, but oh, how I want to go home ...") while we hand rolled our own cigarettes and sipped something they called "acme medicine" out of a jar. (Don't ask!)

I did go to the top of the mountain a few times to recruit children for our Vacation Bible School, but I was uncomfortable going there. That was where the "sorrys" lived. Even they called themselves sorrys and their existence was just that: sorry. I was not afraid of them. They were not mean-spirited people or dangerous, but they lived in total poverty. There was some inbreeding with its perilous complications. An occasional child would be born with multiple medical issues. I have no idea how those people survived. They were so afraid of the world that they did not care to venture down to the bottom of the hollow, where the goods and the get-alongs lived. When we were in a position to offer them groceries, they were afraid to get them. They either sent a more secure teenager or waited for someone from the church to bring the supplies up. The goods and the get-alongs liked to sit on their porches in the evenings, watching the cars drive up that coal town road. The sorrys stayed inside, afraid and embarrassed.

Toward the end of the summer of 1968, as I was hitchhiking up a rural road, I caught a ride with a coal miner in his pickup truck. "What ya do for a living, boy?" he asked bluntly.

Affecting the local dialect and vocabulary, I said, "Well, sir, I'm gonna make a preacher." (That's Appalachian for "studying for the ordained ministry.")

"Make a preacher?" he whooped. "Land o' Goshen, boy. Don't you know you are going to starve to death? Ain't nobody goes to church no more. The whole church thing is goin' outta business. Now, you go out there and find yourself a real job. Boy like you needs to make something of hisself; not make a preacher."

As I stepped down from the truck, I expressed my gratitude for his advice and promised to consider it. Of course, I did not do as he suggested, but I was shocked and not awed. I had thought I was doing something wonderful and he was telling me I was a wastrel and a fool, throwing my life away.

While I did not follow his advice, he did do two things for me: he was the first disinterested and impartial observer I met who told me that the church was dying and maybe, more significantly, he crushed any self-importance right out of me. Any clergyperson who takes himself or herself too seriously needs to have an encounter with an Appalachian coal miner. That man spoke great truths. The church lives on the ragged edge. As with skilled construction workers on high-rise office buildings, it is possible to build something magnificent, but with one misstep, a church can doom its very existence. If you pick any era of history in the past two thousand years, you will find brilliant and knowledgeable people proclaiming the church's death. As far back as the fifth century, St. Augustine wrote his epic *The City of God* because he was sure the sack of Rome was a harbinger of the death of the church. But it survived. Those death knells never stop ringing.

Contrary to the standards of most of American culture, Christianity is not about being a hit with the public. While the church must be shrewd and attentive to what is going on around it, it will never succeed by market surveys, focus groups, and mass advertising. Every attempt to be on the cutting edge ends up being out of date within a short period of time. I still think about those goods and get-alongs sitting quietly on their porches in the evenings. Christianity is about being, living, waiting, and responding. It is about letting something mystical, mysterious, and holy fill the empty places between your hopes and your dreams. It is about listening, remembering, and praying.

I had some good times among the people of Avondale hollow. I knew their music and their simple aspirations and we spent a lot of time in innocent friendship. The children loved Vacation Bible School and the parents were happy to jump in and help out with the program, but I had never experienced poverty like that before in America and I am sure I never will again.

REFINDING MY SOUL MATE

Through those first two years of seminary, I missed Ellen. As I said, she went to Louisville to teach in 1966. While she was there, she decided she wanted to earn a Master's degree in Latin. She applied to Tufts University in Medford, Massachusetts, just outside of Boston. The program started with one year of study and research in Naples, Italy. The second year was in residence on the campus of Tufts. So, in the fall of 1966, she took off for what proved to be a delightful year in Italy with OPM (That stands for a full scholarship, or "other people's money"!). In 1967, she returned to America to complete her work. I was in the second of my three years in seminary while she was in Medford. Somehow, I learned where she was and thought I would try to see if she might give me one more chance. I did the preposterous thing of writing to her, addressed to the Classics department of Tufts University. A minor miracle - the letter actually got to her. I have no idea what I said, but it must have been compelling, because she wrote back and within no time at all our relationship was flourishing far more joyfully than the first time around.

I remember going to Medford in February, 1968. How could I forget? The snow poured down; my little Volkswagen Beetle got plowed into a bank of snow and I wondered if I would ever get home. A second trip in the spring ended up being the same weekend Martin Luther King Jr. was assassinated. As I was driving south through Maryland and eastern Washington, DC, angry, militant African Americans were burning Washington. Traveling along the Anacostia Freeway, I saw the smoke from burning buildings drifting around me.

As soon as I thought it was appropriate, I proposed to her and she said yes. It was probably hard for her to understand what she meant to me. She was my sanity and equilibrium in a world that was going crazy. In 1968, Bobby Kennedy and Martin Luther King Jr. were both assassinated. The Tet Offensive in Vietnam was devastating America's military confidence. People marched on the Pentagon by the thousands, and the riots of the hippies at the Democratic National Convention and the violent response of the Chicago police were both tragic. I walked the streets of Washington after the Martin Luther King Jr. riots practically in tears. The world was going to hell, but somehow, it seemed to me that Ellen and I could weather these turbulent times and end up having an abundant life. My faith was in Ellen.

I did not want to waste a moment. I wanted her with me for my last year in seminary. We set August 31, 1968 as the date for our wedding, right after my foray into McDowell County. This is not to say that getting married was easy. There was nothing easy about it. We had a modest wedding in St. Paul's Church in Pittsburgh, with a fruit punch and cookies reception in the church's parish hall. By the way, the police riot in Chicago was going on while we were having our reception. People stood there and watched it on television. We did not care. We were married and on our way to a life together. Our official honeymoon was two nights at the Bedford Springs Inn in central Pennsylvania. We had to get on our way back to Alexandria because she had been hired to teach Latin at Mt. Vernon High School. In 1970, we had what we called our "real honeymoon" when we spent a few weeks in England and then connected with Bob and Susan Hardman for the first of what became our many trips to France.

ENDING SEMINARY

My last year in seminary was delightful. Ellen and I rented a log cabin in the woods with a pond in front of it. It was just a mile or two away the seminary. We often would have parties there. In the dead of winter, we ice skated on the pond. I was elected the senior class president. Something I did not realize at the time; if you are elected the senior class president, you stay president for the rest of your life. That suited me just fine. I love my classmates, every one of them. I love staying in touch with them. Even after all these years, I still represent my class at official seminary activities.

I had a fieldwork job at St. John's Church, located on Lafayette Square in Washington, DC. Known as "The Church of the Presidents," it was amazing. One author once called it one of the "five truly cardinal parishes" in America." [17] I am not sure I know exactly what a cardinal parish is. All I know is that this one was impressive. The rector, John Harper, was a Harvard graduate who had known President Kennedy in college. He was handsome, articulate, and perfectly designed for that congregation. I worked with some other seminarians who have remained dear friends throughout our lives: Peter Kreitler, Pickett Miles, Clem Jordan, Mike Vermillion, and I were joined by the freshly minted ordinand Peter Lee, the Assistant Rector. It was Peter's job to keep us focused. Forget it. We all loved poking fun at the pretensions of this upper-class congregation; we certainly were not going to be pushed into a mold that John Harper or Peter Lee thought we needed to assume. Peter went on to have a distinguished career in the Episcopal Church. Eventually, he became one of America's greatest bishops. Even back then, it was clear to me that he was destined for greatness.

Over the years, I have spent no small amount of time contemplating the ministry of John Harper. Like many clergy, he was a complicated man, but he was a gift to that highly influential congregation. He was erudite, well-read, sophisticated, and a brilliant preacher. He was hard to know, and at times, I felt as if I wanted to scold him for the cavalier way he treated some of his parishioners. But I watched him closely

---

[17] Kit Konolige, *The Power of their Glory: America's Ruling Class, the Episcopalians.* Wyden Press, a division of Simon and Schuster: New York (1978)

and tried to emulate the things he did well and understand the things I did not like.

GETTING STARTED

Early in 1969, I found out that I was going to be assigned a church in Summersville, West Virginia. That was how they did things back then. If one was accepted by a bishop for ordination, that bishop had the right to assign the person anywhere he wished. Just think about this: Ellen had lived in Pittsburgh, Louisville, Naples, Boston, and Alexandria, and now I was telling her we were going to Summersville. We got out an atlas and the town was not on the map. The bishop, Wilburn C. Campbell, was not the kind of man to apologize for anything, but he sort of apologized. He explained to me that there were no openings in the diocese and he did not want to lose me to another diocese. He assured me that as soon as some other church opened up, he would relocate me. Looking back at some of those indentured servants in my ancient past, I understood what was going on. I was an indentured servant of the Bishop of West Virginia. Until I served under him long enough to pay off my scholarship debts, I was his property.

So on St. Barnabas Day, June 11, 1969, I was ordained a Transitional Deacon at St. John's Church, Charleston.[18] Immediately after that, we moved into the vicarage of St. Martin's-in-the-Fields Episcopal Church. I was paid one hundred and fifty dollars per month, plus housing and fifty

---

[18] A Transitional Deacon is a person who is heading toward ordination as a Priest; a Vocational Deacon is a person whose ordination process terminates at that point.

dollars a month for automobile expenses. (And, as Mike Vermillion said, "all the Gideon Bibles I could eat.") I have no idea how we survived financially. Ellen did some substitute teaching and that helped make ends meet. One Sunday, a month or so after I arrived, there were nine people in church, including Ellen and me, her visiting parents, and the organist. Only four other lonely souls ventured out. Of course, this was just after all the glitz and glamour of jam-packed St. John's Lafayette Square! The Senior Warden, that is, the parishioner elected to work with the clergyperson to help fulfill the mission of the church, refused to do a thing. I called my first Vestry meeting for August and he did not bother to come. He said he did not go out at night, and besides, I was the one being paid, not him. There was a sort of unelected Senior Warden, a local attorney named John Breckenridge, who was a gracious man, willing to give a raw Vicar a hand.

I was in shell shock! I had spent all of that time training to be a clergyman and this was it? One day, I walked into the bank to attend to some business. The president of the bank, a thirty-something man, welcomed me and began to engage in a chatty conversation. After all, I was a new customer and he was anxious to get to know me. He said, "Say, I hear you have just graduated from one of them-there seminar schools over in Virginia. That sounds pretty great."

I thought, *Them-there seminar schools?* Was it possible that the president of the bank was so educationally limited that he did not know the word was seminary? Yes, it was possible!

While I did not want to stay there any longer than I had to, there were some bright spots. Ellen had gone back to Tufts to put the finishing touches on her Master's that summer, so I was on my own. The wife of the church's treasurer, Janet Jarrell, and her sisters had just opened an Italian restaurant. It quickly became identified as one of the top restaurants in the state by food critics. At their insistence, every evening I would go down to the restaurant before the regular dinner crowd arrived and they would feed me for free. They were sweet people and the meals were amazing.

In Summersville, I had what I call my second revelatory experience of God. This was the time when I really began to grasp the personal nature of God. One day, I was sitting in my office when the phone rang. A man and a woman were out on the edge of town in a restaurant. They were traveling through and they wanted to know if I could come to the restaurant to talk. When I got there, they told me that their teenage son, who was in a hospital for the chronically ill, was dying. A "chronically ill hospital" was a nice name for a place for those who had run out of medical options. When this boy was about six, an automobile had struck him. From that time forward, he had been in a chronic vegetative state. They asked if I would go give him last rites. "Of course," I said.

The hospital was about forty miles away. It was a state-owned facility for those who could not afford private care. We drove in separate cars. On the way over, I felt almost enfolded by a kind of warmth, light, and peace that I could not ever recall experiencing before. Then, when I got to his room, I was distressed. Here was this child with the body of a six-year-old and the head of a teenager curled up in a fetal position. He had a heart monitor on and it was pounding at twice the speed of a normal heartbeat. His body temperature was highly elevated. His mother said, "Jim, will you pray for his healing?"

Oh my God. Was she serious? Couldn't she just let her poor little son slip away? Of course, I was going to honor her request. To tell the truth, I did not even want to touch him, but I did. I rested my hand on his forehead. My heart was not in my prayer, but I did pray that God would heal this child. Within about a minute, his heartbeat settled down to a normal rate and he broke out into perspiration as his temperature lowered to normal. His parents smiled happily as if they had expected nothing less. I was agog. He lived a couple more years and finally, his fragile body wore out. I believe that God was saying to Jim Sell that God's agenda will never be Jim Sell's agenda and that God's timing will always be out of my control. At best, Jim Sell will never be anything more than one who stands in awe of God's mighty works.

On December 19, 1969, with two others, Art Bennett and Curt Cowell, I was ordained a Priest at St. Stephen's Episcopal Church in Beckley. I was honored that John Harper came over to be the preacher.

CHRIST CHURCH, WILLIAMSTOWN

The following February, after a mere eight months in Summersville, a clergy vacancy opened at Christ Episcopal Church, Williamstown, West Virginia. Faithful to his word, the bishop shuttled me over there right away. Williamstown is actually a suburb of Marietta, Ohio, and a good portion of the congregation drove across the Ohio River Bridge to attend church there. While it too was a small congregation, it was at least ten times larger than St. Martin's-in-the-Fields.

The church is a sweet little stone building with a nave that probably holds about one hundred people. There were two different congregations when I arrived which were somewhat intermingled. There were the long term Williamstown residents who had belonged to the church for most of their lives. Then there were a considerable number of young adults who had moved in more recently.

First, I want to share a few remembrances of the natives. They were welcoming of Ellen and me. June Wilson was particularly memorable. We had been there for a couple of days, when there was a knock on our front door. Ellen and I both went to answer it. There was June, holding a beautiful lemon meringue pie. She was gracious as she said, "I want you to know how very happy my husband, daughter, and I are that you are here. We hope you have a good stay with us, but there is something you need to understand. This is our church. It is the church of this congregation. We will be here long after you leave. We want you to give us leadership, and we want to be fed by you, but we know you must be transitional, and we must be the permanent body of Christ." She was correct and we thanked her for her wisdom. We never forgot her words. We kept them in mind wherever we went. The congregation is the church. The clergyperson is just passing through.

When I tell my colleagues that I have taken loaded guns away from three of my parishioners, they usually gasp in amazement. A frightened or angry person with a weapon who might have been drinking is always serious business and not something to be taken lightly. The first time was in Williamstown. The second time was in Lewisburg. The third was in Norfolk. However, in every case, it was not as dramatic as it might sound. With the first two, it was the result of a domestic quarrel. In both instances, the husband, who was holding the gun, gave his wife permission to call me and ask me to come over. The gun in question in Williamstown was a little "Saturday night special" that he was waving around. When I asked him to give it to me, he did so readily and, I think, was relieved that he had a comfortable way to defuse the situation. In Lewisburg, it was a shotgun. Again, the husband was quietly appreciative that he had the opportunity to bring some sanity to his own behavior. As far as I know, both couples got help from counselors and continued to live together successfully as husband and wife. The third time, a colleague and I went to talk to a parishioner who had killed a man in a street fight. He was ready to surrender and we supported him through his arrest, trial and incarceration. I am glad I never had to do that chore again! I also think that the quiet, cool compassion of an experienced clergyperson can have a more healing effect in such potentially dangerous situations than the "swat team" approach of some law enforcement organizations. But from that time on, I have prayed that America would alter the Second Amendment to the Constitution. I especially resonate with the recent suggestion of retired Supreme Court Justice John Paul Stevens,[19] who proposes that we simply add five words to the Second Amendment to permit arms "when serving in the militia." That seems to have been our forbearer's intention at the beginning. I know such a suggestion is dead on arrival in today's NRA-infused culture. Gun violence has grown to become, as H. Rap Brown, the Black Panther member, once called it, "as American as cherry pie." I have faith that someday a wiser attitude toward gun ownership will come to pass.

---

[19] John Paul Stevens, *Six Amendments: How And Why We Should Change the Constitution*, Little, Brown: New York (2013)

There was one man in Christ Church's congregation who stood out and still stands out in my mind even to this day. His name is Brent Biddle. Do not be confused. He was not some Philadelphia blueblood. Maybe he was a distant relative of the famous Biddles of Philadelphia, but in fact, he was a modest tomato farmer. After a certain period of time, when he thought he could trust me, he came by and said he wanted to talk. Actually, he had several stories to tell, but one I remember with great clarity. He was the first person I ever knew who had had what later became known as a life-after-life experience. He felt as if he had entered the world of the dying and dead and returned. Brent's story was so simple and straightforward that I believed every word of it, even to this day. He had been hospitalized in Marietta Memorial Hospital. One evening, the Vicar of the church, Charlie McNutt, and Brent's wife were called to come. The doctor said he would not last the night. Brent reported that he lay there in something like a coma. Suddenly, he found himself outside of his body, looking down on the room. He saw his wife and Charlie in prayer. Then he turned, as if toward heaven, and saw a warm, attractive light. He felt as if he were being pulled toward the light. He entered it and as he did so, he was met by his deceased mother who asked him if he wanted to come with her. He said he did and he was looking forward to it, but then she said that it was not his time. He needed to go back to care for his wife and daughter. In a moment, he was back in his mortal body and he awakened. His wife and Charlie were surprised to see that he was suddenly feeling better and they were relieved. Two days later, he was feeling well enough to go home.

Had this story been told to me by someone else, I might have been somewhat skeptical, but there was no man more honest on the face of the earth that Brent Biddle. About five years later, a University of Virginia professor named Raymond Moody wrote a book in which he described the same kind of event that Brent had experienced.[20] When the Moody book was published and was something of a best seller, I just smiled and said, "Oh yes. I am very familiar with those experiences."

There was a whole other population in the Williamstown church that was substantially different but comfortably integrated into the wider congregation. For such a small church, there was a sizable population of young adults. Many of them lived in Marietta and just liked the neighborly ambience of this West Virginia church. They immediately took Ellen and me in and treated us as members of their informal young adult group. It was not uncommon for several young wives to call around to each other and say, "Hey, what's for dinner tonight?" We would meet at someone's home and have dinner. Each couple would scrounge around their kitchen and find something to share. We were all pretty poor and the sharing not only made a difference financially, but it was great fun.

One young couple ended up being lifelong friends. In September, 1971, newly married Maggie and Nick Miles showed up in church. They had rented a modest garage apartment down the street and were looking for a church. Of course, they were made to feel welcome by the old-timers and the young adults alike. Shortly thereafter, it looked as if Nick might get drafted. He made the decision to enlist in the army and volunteered to

---

[20] Raymond Moody, *Life After Life: The Investigation of a Phenomenon - Survival of Bodily Death,* Mockingbird Books: Fairhope Alabama (1975).

be a medic. Off to Texas he went to be trained. Maggie stayed behind because she was teaching kindergarten. Ellen was teaching English at Marietta High School, so the two women were professionally connected. One night, around dinnertime, the phone rang. It was Maggie. She said to me, "Would you mind coming over to my apartment? I am feeling a little scared."

I scurried over there. It was an unusually cold night in April and the apartment was chilly. She said, "When I got home, a window was open. I think somebody has been in here."

I said, "I will wait for you. Gather up what you need. You are coming to spend the night at our house." She never went back to the apartment except with Ellen or me to close it up. She was our guest for about six weeks until she moved to Texas to join Nick. That time together cemented a relationship, especially between Ellen and Maggie. Maggie is the sister Ellen never had, and they continue to connect and be mutually supportive after all these years. When I think about life in the church, I think about the many friends we made, such as Maggie and Nick, whom we feel blessed to have had come our way. They went on to have wonderful careers, traveling throughout the world, but they still remain part of our family. As a postscript, I recall how, some years later, after careful plotting on Maggie's part, they showed up in Chartres, France, from Italy, where they were living, completely unannounced when they knew that we were going to be there. That is the kind of friends they are.

JAMES ANDREW SELL

I want to share a final important remembrance about Williamstown. Ellen and I had been married three years and felt we were ready to have a child. Before we knew it, Ellen was pregnant. On a cold night in February, during the 1972 Winter Olympics, Ellen announced that it was time for us to go to the hospital. She never forgot watching me fill up on Chef Boyardee ravioli directly from the can while she was getting dressed to go. All I could think about was that I did not know the next time I would have a meal and at two in the morning I figured I better fortify myself.

She was in labor for a long time. She and I had completed the Lamaze training for childbirth and I would help coach her in their recommended breathing techniques, which were intended to ease the pain of delivery. When it was time for the baby to be born, it was as if we were in the Middle Ages. Fathers were not allowed in the delivery room back then. Ellen's obstetrician was afraid that I might pass out cold and he would not have time to attend to me. So I stood outside the delivery room with the door cracked open, watching the entire delivery through a window in the door.

I had a pretty good view. Back then, there was no way of knowing what the gender of the baby was until it was born. We had names for either eventuality. When James Andrew came into the world, he arrived with his eyes wide open. His birth was the most sacred moment of my life up to that time. I felt as if I had discovered something that no one else in the world knew about; the miracle of birth. An ecstatic experience is one where a person is taken out of his or her body into a heavenly place. I had the ecstatic experience of watching Ellen bring Andrew into the world. My love for Ellen was overflowing and my love for Andrew was instantaneous.

And so the third James Sell was born. Each James Sell was unique, but we are all deeply connected. My father was James

Nathaniel. I am James William Henry, named after my father and my two grandfathers and my son is James Andrew. I used to tell people we named him Andrew after the wondrous saint who was the first apostle and the big, hulking brother of St. Peter, but the truth is that we just liked the name. Rather than force him to bear the burden of being another James Sell, we elected to call him Andrew.

CHAPTER 3

KNOWING THE BOUNDARIES

Each Wednesday, I would go to Trinity Church in Parkersburg, West Virginia, to help the rector, Griff Callahan. I would usually take the midweek service, visit a few people in their homes and make the rounds of the hospitals. Between Parkersburg and Williamstown, I was beginning to get the hang of Episcopal ministry.

This practice seems pretty antiquated these days, but throughout my years in West Virginia and well into my ministry in Sparta, New Jersey, it was common for the minister to drop in uninvited on people at their homes late in the afternoons and early evenings. There was usually no agenda other than to be a presence in their lives. Not infrequently, matters of pastoral concern would come up. However, we were not there to pry. That particular practice began to come to an end in the late 1970s and early '80s, when a number of clergy began acting out inappropriately. This behavior was identified as especially egregious in some Roman Catholic situations where priests were identified as pedophiles. My notion about Episcopal clergy was that when incidents happened, they were more about adult-to-adult sexual misconduct. There was one moment, unique in the history of humankind, when sexual behavior had no external barriers or sanctions. Between the advent of the birth control pill and the coming of the AIDS epidemic, sexual misconduct could be free of reproductive or medical consequences. Families could be destroyed and personal integrity could go down the drain, but unwanted pregnancies could be avoided and there was no threat of terminal illness. Rumors were rife and often had some basis in fact. It all ground to a halt with the AIDS epidemic and the demands of the women's movement not to put up with unlevel playing fields. Because of the heightened anxieties over these malfeasances, I ceased most visitations in homes except in the case of a death in the family. My decision to end home visits was more about the perception than anything else. I did not need to be seen coming out of some home alone and have neighbors conjecture about my presence there. Even in family crises, I made sure I was not alone with another person. If I received a call after hours from a person who needed to talk, I would meet the individual some place like a late-night diner or other safe venue. In like manner, I did not have people come to my office unless a secretary or other staff person was close by. Usually, I kept the door slightly ajar if it did not have a glass panel in it. It was simple to explain to the parishioners what I was doing and they always understood.

LEWISBURG, WEST VIRGINIA

To say that I always wanted to live in Lewisburg was not far from the truth. When I was a young child, we would drive the hundred miles east of Charleston on twisting, mountainous U.S. Route 60 to Lewisburg to attend the West Virginia State Fair just outside of that town. The Greenbrier Valley is, arguably, the most beautiful part of West Virginia. It is a wide

open land of bluegrass with gorgeous farms. To the east of it
are the mountains of the Eastern Divide on the border with
Virginia. To the west, the mountains enfold the Gauley River
National Recreation Area, with its churning river rapids, which
make it exciting to the adventuresome. I had gone to two Boy
Scout camps in Greenbrier County. On was located in a little
crossroads called Sunlight, which is now a ghost town, and the
other in a state park called Bluebend. Lewisburg seemed to call
out to me with an unceasing siren song.

In the 1950s, Griff Callahan began resurrecting the
Episcopal ministry in Lewisburg, which had completely died
out during World War II. There had been two churches of long
standing in White Sulfur Springs and another in Ronceverte.
However, the Episcopal presence in Lewisburg had frittered
away, so a sweet little brick church was built in a residential
neighborhood and they reclaimed their old name of St. James
Church. After Griff, Harold Hendricks, Clifford Shane and
David Jones served as Vicars. All of them did good jobs and
strengthened the struggling little Episcopal community.

I had known David Jones since college. He and I were
in the same fraternity. He is everything I want a priest to be:
conscientious, faith-filled, hardworking and attentive to people.
He went to Lewisburg right out of seminary in 1968. While
he was there, the church built a nice, comfortable rectory. He
developed a thriving ministry to the students at Greenbrier
Military School and Greenbrier College for Women. In the
natural order of things, after four years, he was called to St.
Stephen's in Beckley. Immediately, I let the Bishop know that
I would be interested in following him. This kind of rapid
transition would never happen today, but only one week lapsed

between Dave's departure and my arrival. Parenthetically, Dave went on to have a successful career and was a distinguished Suffragan Bishop in the Diocese of Virginia with my old colleague Peter Lee, who was the head bishop of that diocese.

Ellen put up with a lot in being my wife. Perhaps our most difficult times were when we made a move to a new community. She would get planted in the old community, get a teaching job and settle in for the long haul. Then I would come along and say that we were moving and the announcement would produce a kind of pandemonium in her that took a long time to work through. Such was the move from Williamstown to Lewisburg. She loved Williamstown, with our tight little group of young adult friends and her job in Marietta, so she was frustrated by the move. Andrew was just a few weeks old when we left. We got through it, and soon enough, she was fully transplanted to our new home.

Getting there was a story unto itself. There was a mover in nearby Ronceverte named Buzzy Allen. He came over to Williamstown and loaded us up. On the day of the move, Ellen and I left together. She drove one Volkswagen Beetle and I drove the other. She took off with baby Andrew and I followed with Pepper, our black schnauzer dog. As we crossed the center of the state on U.S. Route 60, we went over Sewell Mountain, through a little town called Ansted. She was in front and never saw that my car broke down. It had thrown a rod, which is a devastating thing to go wrong. I limped over to the side of the road as she roared on down the highway. Carrying Pepper, I walked a mile or so to a garage. The mechanic was having his lunch and he was not going to pay any attention to me while he was on his break. After an hour or so, he finally drove me back to the car, where he pronounced it seriously broken. I had no one I could call, no phone numbers and no way of finding help. Of course, we had not had a phone installed in the new house yet. Not having any choice, I found a piece of rope to make a leash and began to hitchhike. After another hour or so, a young couple saw me with my black schnauzer and stopped. They had a salt and pepper schnauzer and had never seen an all-black one, so out of curiosity, they picked me up and drove me the last hour and a half to the outskirts of Lewisburg. Pepper and I walked to our new home from there. A few days later, I went back, emptied the car of my luggage and sold it on the spot. Ta-da! That was my grand entrance into the town of Lewisburg. By the way, Buzzy became our trusted mover for years into the future, relocating us or my father four or five more times until he died in an accident on his travels.

I ended up being in Lewisburg for eight years. To tell the truth, it never entered my mind that I was going to be there that long. Two separate realities came to bear in that tenure. First of all, we liked living there and felt included in the life of the community. Secondly, I had a hard time convincing congregations that I might be a suitable candidate for their churches because I was living in my third little rural village in West Virginia. They assumed I was not ready for prime time. I was dismissed before I was even seriously considered.

I simply did not care about looking around. America was still in the throes of Vietnam and the national polarization it produced. Ellen and I were just happy to get away from all of that thunder and lightning and find a place where we could settle down, raise a family and be deeply connected to one another.

I never anticipated that throughout Greenbrier and Monroe counties, a whole lot of young people were moving onto small subsistence farms to engage in a kind of modern homesteading life. They called themselves earthals, as they sought to live off the earth as much as possible. The locals described them as burned-out hippies who were fed up with urban living and were seeking a more tranquil experience. The joke was "Do you know how to tell a local farmer from an earthal farmer? A local farmer gets drunk and falls off his tractor. An earthal farmer is different. An earthal gets stoned and falls of his tractor." These were a new breed of people. Many were well-educated. Some brought exceptional artistic skills with them. They sought to live frugally and with an environmental consciousness. They bent over backward to be good neighbors to the natives as they began to introduce us to things like unprocessed foods, organic gardening, community activism, and cottage industries.

In many ways, Ellen and I could relate to these people. While we came across as the WASP[21] Episcopalians we were, we shared many of their values and history. A large number of them gave up after a year or two of struggling on the land and sought other lives in other places. But many of them stayed on, put down roots and moved into the mainstream of the community. Despite their ways, these new residents ended up bringing a whole new style of living to the valley. If you go to Lewisburg today, you will find a town filled with all kinds of artists and crafts persons. There are painters, potters, artisans, actors and musicians. In 2012, a national travel magazine called Lewisburg the "coolest small town in America." It is a justly

---

[21] *WASP* is an acronym for "White Anglo-Saxon Protestant".

earned title, and the transformation began in the early '70s with the arrival of the earthals.

However, there was more to Lewisburg than just arts and crafts. In 1972, Greenbrier Military School (GMS) shut its doors and went out of business. Within a matter of months, the Greenbrier College of Osteopathic Medicine began its program in the old GMS buildings. Today, Lewisburg is probably the smallest town in America with its own medical school. They train over one hundred and fifty students per year to serve in medical practices in rural communities. This annual influx of well-educated young adults, with their need for housing and a social life, has been a financial windfall to the town, as well as a source of ongoing energy.

The same year GMS closed, the Greenbrier College for Women also closed. This school had been a junior college that offered programs for high school girls in their junior and senior years and for freshmen and sophomores in college. In its place, the State of West Virginia opened the Greenbrier Center, a residential facility for mentally challenged children. Some years later, the facility morphed into a highly successful community college. These institutions bring some accomplished educators to the town who add richly to the community mix.

And of course, there is The Greenbrier. Located on six thousand acres ten miles east of Lewisburg in the town of White Sulfur Springs, the Greenbrier is a hotel that is unparalleled in its sophistication and amenities. When we arrived, they had three golf courses and perhaps six hundred rooms. It was and is world famous. The dining is incomparable and the service is breathtaking. Because it housed a Cold War era bunker suitable for wartime protection for Federal government officials, the local airport had the longest runway in the state, assuring access from Washington, D.C. The hotel went on to create something called the Sporting Club, which is a growing community of upscale homes for highly successful people who wish to add a trophy residence to their portfolios. The Sporting Club has its own golf course and a wide array of private attractions.

The Federal Women's Reformatory was in Alderson. It was the eventual home of such people as Tokyo Rose and Axis Sally, both World War II war criminals, as well as two women who attempted to assassinate presidents, Lynette "Squeaky" Frome and Sara Jane Moore, not to mention a whole lot of other notorious ladies. While it was about twenty-five miles from Lewisburg, some of its top administrators and professionals either lived in Lewisburg or used the town as the center of their lives. One of my Senior Wardens, Virginia McLaughlin, was the warden of the penitentiary. I called her the warden of the "big house" (the prison) by day and warden of the "little house" (the church) by night.

Finally, I need to mention the coal industry. There has never been any coal in the limestone substructure of eastern Greenbrier County, but a number of senior executives in the industry elected to live there and commute west to their mines, often more than fifty miles away. Making the commute in their personal helicopters was not unheard of.

The mix of ideas, energy, financial resources, creativity and skills produced a unique community filled with people living productive lives. It might have been rural, but it was more sophisticated than one could possibly imagine.

Prayer Book Revision

The principal forms of worship in the Episcopal Church have always derived from something called the Book of Common Prayer. This is a book that was initially developed by a man named Thomas Cranmer during the English Reformation in the 1600s. He translated the Roman Catholic monastic worship known as matins into English from Latin and called it Morning Prayer. Next, he gave the Catholic Mass a unique Anglican and Protestant slant and called it Holy Communion. Then he created services for the sacraments, including baptism, marriage, burial, and confirmation. Before the American Revolution, Episcopalians used the version of the Prayer Book which was the standard at the time in England. Actually, we were still called Anglicans through the Revolution. When the war ended, things English were looked upon as unpatriotic, so we changed our name to Episcopalians, meaning "having bishops."

From the Church of England's earliest time, there was an expectation that as history and theology evolved, the Prayer Book would be modified and edited to stay consistent with contemporary policy and practice. After the Revolution, we first deleted prayers on behalf of King George. Later, we created editions that met the needs of the time. Toward the end of the nineteenth century, one new Prayer Book was adopted. However, World War I was an enormous game changer in church life. Much of that Prayer Book was seen as being overly judgmental and lacking in grace by the 1920s "lost generation" of veterans. Therefore, the leadership of the Episcopal Church began a process of revision. Something called the Standing Liturgical Commission was established. In 1928, they published a trial version of a Prayer Book that successfully addressed many of the concerns of the clergy and laity. Without further ado, they adopted it as the official Prayer Book. These were the forms of worship that I grew up on as a child, studied in seminary and with which I launched the early years of my ministry. There is no question that worship from that book was inspirational. The Elizabethan language was lyrical and soaring. When those words were spoken by an elegant male baritone priest, we felt as if we were at the portals of heaven.

Just as World War I changed the way Episcopalians perceived God's mighty acts, World War II was even more unsettling for us. People were looking for worship that was more clearly stated and less formal. Church attendance was at an all-time high and churches were becoming the gathering points for many communities. In the 1950s and '60s, the great polarization among Episcopalians was between the Anglo-Catholic High Church worshipers, who emphasized the sacraments, and the Low Church Protestant worshipers who felt that Bible reading and preaching should be primary. In the early '60s, a small group of clergy and laity informally began to explore avenues of worship that these two polar groups might find mutually attractive. Also, in the mid-1960s, the Roman Catholic Church's Second Vatican Council undertook a major update and revision of their worship. We listened to their conversations and took some of their best ideas for ourselves.

Thus, in the late 1960s, the Standing Liturgical Commission began a long and complicated process of preparing a new Prayer Book. When I was still in seminary, the first iteration was introduced. In the following years, there would be additional forms. Perhaps the most surprising change was that many of the worship services were offered in two linguistic styles. One (Rite I) was classic Elizabethan English, similar to the King James Bible and the 1928 Prayer Book. The other (Rite II) was contemporary twentieth century language. The National Council of Churches was introducing well-researched new translations of the Bible that were also in a contemporary idiom. These two publications paired well together. It was clear to anyone who had an interest in evangelism and church growth that the contemporary language version was intended as the principal form of worship. Newcomers found Elizabethan language awkward and arcane. If one wanted to encourage and welcome prospective members, it was important that the contemporary language worship be used. After more than forty years of practice, I see a continuing ebbing of Rite I's use. Many churches seem to use Rite II at all services, unless they are adventuring into even more timely settings. Being the old Episcopalian that I am, I appreciate those remaining few worshipers whose spirit soars from the old Elizabethan language. I still feel the rapture of a classic sung Evensong in Rite I language on a late Sunday afternoon with a full choir of men, women, boys and girls.

A more substantial change in the new Prayer Book was that it made the Holy Eucharist[22] the central act of all worship. This modification was going back to Christianity's earliest roots and was consistent with biblical practice. I had been raised in the tradition where the Morning Prayer service with a sermon was seen as the standard Sunday morning worship offering.

---

[22] *Holy Eucharist*, a more historically inclusive term than *Holy Communion* or *Mass*, was popularized at that time, derived from the Greek word for "thanksgiving."

Even though I was convinced of the wisdom of this change, it was still hard for me. After a lifetime of Morning Prayer seasoned with occasional Holy Communion, switching to an all Communion practice took some getting used to. It was probably harder for the people of Lewisburg, because most of them had also come out of that Low Church history as well. But together we weathered the change and were the better for it. On December 1, 1976, a UPS truck rolled up to St. James Church and delivered cases of the new Prayer Book. The books were still in trial use and this was the first day we were allowed to use them. We had been through years of experimentation and knew the die was cast. We all decided that we might as well get on with it from the start. Actually, compared to some places where the clergy and other leadership might have waffled, we had a fairly easy time of it.

ORDAINING WOMEN

At about the same time that we were considering new Prayer Books, something of far greater substance was in the works. I guess I missed reading Betty Friedan's *The Feminine Mystique* because I first became aware of the subject of women's rights when I picked up a copy of *Esquire* magazine in the mid-1960s that contained an extended piece on the subject. The subject it raised caused me to reconsider practically everything I thought about the relationships between men and women. Within a matter of weeks, I came to see that the issues being debated were legitimate. If we meant it when we said that "all men are created equal," that statement had to include all men and women.

I was born and raised in a church that only let males have leadership roles. From the acolytes or altar boys who assisted the clergy in worship to the members of the clergy and vestry, office holders and leaders were all male. That began to change in the early '60s. My mother nominated the first woman to her church's vestry back then. The congregations I served in the early 1970s were so small that it never entered my mind not to use girls as acolytes. We simply did not have enough boys to go around. However, the idea of ordaining women was a whole different concept. The argument from the earliest days was that Jesus had only called men into leadership and things had to stay that way. There had been a few occasions when women managed to be ordained in Protestant churches, but basically, no church that had what was known as "apostolic succession"[23] - and those churches made up almost all of worldwide Christianity - had ever even dreamed of ordaining women. When eleven women who had been theologically trained talked three Episcopal bishops into ordaining them in an unauthorized service in Philadelphia on July 27, 1974, the outcry was international. One of the leaders of this group is a dear friend of mine, the Rev. Alison Cheek, my only classmate to end up with her picture on the cover of *Time* magazine. Alison was not one to be seen as an earth shaker, but she was strong enough to endure the slings and arrows that were flung at her. Living in West Virginia, I was pretty much out of the center of church politics and did not even know this was being talked about before it happened. One of my regrets is that I could not claim that I was there at that historic occasion. For a few months, the Episcopal Church

---

[23] Bishops in direct succession from St. Peter, the first bishop of the church: that is, the Anglican, Orthodox and Roman Catholic denominations.

tried to sort things out. In the end, they approved the concept of the ordination of women and regularized the ordinations of Alison and her sister co-conspirators. Perhaps this is a story of the tail wagging the dog. Two and a half million Episcopalians did something at least two billion other Christians around the world had never considered doing.

My first close encounter with the process of a woman's ordination came along a few years later. I first met Betsy Walker when she was in the eighth grade. Bright, artistically talented, and a ball of fire, she kept all of us on our toes. She became involved with the Episcopal Church summer camp and was smitten with the notion of being ordained. I count her as the first of many men and women who were willing to consider ordination at my cautious urging. She ended up being one of the first woman ordained a priest in West Virginia. Currently, she has a valuable career as the head chaplain of the federal reformatory for women in Alderson, West Virginia. Ellen and I attended her wedding to her partner, Pat, a few years ago in Washington, DC. Betsy and Pat Walker have been strong proponents of equal marriage opportunities in the LBGT community of West Virginia. Same sex marriage was legalized there in 2014.

From these initial beginnings, the shape of the Episcopal ministry was altered forever. Today, some of our seminaries consist of almost all female students. Eventually, the entire Anglican Communion came along and followed our lead. Of course, the Roman Catholics continue to be unable to step forward and broaden their priesthood. And the Eastern Orthodox churches do not even know how to discuss it!

The Beginning of a Long
and Difficult Journey

If one were to prioritize the seriousness of the political issues that confronted the church during my professional career, one might think that Prayer Book revision would be near the bottom. Maybe it was, but it was actually near the beginning of a long history of ongoing splintering and division within the denomination. From the test case of a new Prayer Book, one could almost tell how the futures of other political and moral issues were going to break. Most of the scariest chapters of the civil rights era had begun to subside before I was ordained. At least, we were rarely killing and abusing people of color who believed in the dream of civil rights. While there were plenty of recalcitrant Episcopal churches throughout America, by the time I came along, the battle was over, despite the need for years of mopping-up action.

However, people who did not want black worshipers in their congregations were often similar to the same ones who did not want new Prayer Books. Eventually, they seemed to have the same kind of mindset as those who did not want us ordaining women, ordaining gay men and women, consecrating gay bishops or marrying LBGT couples. With every struggle, more and more of the old resistant crowd left. While I personally missed the people I had known for years who splintered off over these issues, I did not miss their narrow-mindedness, lack of vision, failure of nerve, and fear of inclusivity. To tell them that the grace to open one's heart to alienated people was a holy gift of God simply did not work for them. Their hardness of heart was non-negotiable. To be candid, I do not understand how they can have the temerity to call themselves Christians. These people were often insistent that they were persons of faith even when their behavior pointed to something less sincere. Some of my oldest colleagues showed their true colors through these years as they let themselves slip into the dark night of prejudice and spiritual ambiguity. I would rather be a member of a small denomination that is imbued with a sense of justice than the church I was raised in, where decorum and cultural safety eclipsed the opportunity for transformation, spiritual growth, and respect for all of God's people. I am convinced that the remaining elements of the current Episcopal Church will become the foundation of a new, renewed and re-created denomination that believes what it preaches and lives what it teaches.

LEARNING TO LIVE

The people of Lewisburg and St. James Church gave me far more than I ever gave them. There was a certain kind of "from the ground up" decency about them that was not political, economic, or theological. It was the kind of steadfastness and caution people developed as farmers and small-town citizens. Things were not done because they were fashionable. Change came after careful, independent personal consideration. I never watched *The Andy Griffith Show*, so I am not sure that Lewisburg was a parallel universe of Mayberry, but I think it was. Good advice could come from the barber, the gas station attendant, or the neighborhood kid just as well as from the doctor, the lawyer, the merchant or the chief. People listened to one another and grew together as a community. When change came, it was easily incorporated into the fabric of their lives.

Ellen and I were surrounded by many friends and mentors. Libby Dempsey was a singular case in point. Libby had grown up in Christ Church, Ridgewood, New Jersey. Her family had been prosperous but just about went bankrupt with the 1929 stock-market crash and the Great Depression, which were followed by World War II and more struggles. However, each summer, Libby and her family would go to Cape May, New Jersey, and stay in the Chalfont, one of those big, old, airy hotels that are still popular there. While on vacation, they got to know a family from Lewisburg who urged Libby to attend Greenbrier College for Women. In the heart of the war, she applied and was accepted. Not long after arriving, she met a young local veteran, Johnny Dempsey. They married and he started a life insurance business. They had no children. One day, Johnny let her off at the front door of the grocery store and went to park the car. That was the last time she saw him alive. He pulled into a parking spot and had a massive fatal heart attack. I do not think she ever considered returning to New Jersey. She took over Johnny's business and, later, merged it with a group headed by Horace Goodman. Horace was a bona fide saint who cared for Libby and saw that she had the kind of support a young widow in a small town needed.

When we first met her, she was the head of the altar guild and helped provide Sunday evening dinners for the students at the Women's College and the Military School. She wrapped her love around Ellen, Andrew and me. When Katie came along in 1976, Libby was such a part of our family that she became one of Katie's godmothers, along with Todd Ford and Dave Nalker of Lewisburg and Katie's cousin, Anne Chillingworth.

There were a couple of things about Libby that were particularly appealing. First of all, she had a kind of warm, sensitive thoughtfulness that transcended politics or theological perspective. In other words, she was not out to win people over to some particular viewpoint. Being a friend was her highest calling. The church had a Christmas bazaar and a number of people would produce all kinds of crafts for it. Libby was the queen of the bazaar. She would make charming felt Christmas ornaments and decorations that people would line up early to purchase. But she always made sure that she saved some of these special works of art for Andrew and Katie.

Libby did not have a lot of money, but I cannot count the number of times she had us over for dinner. She always liked to use her most beautiful china, silver and crystal that she had received as wedding presents. She loved a formal dinner party and knew that we would be thrilled to be asked. These dinners were always coat and tie affairs. That was the culture of the town. Of course, we always made sure to invite her to special events at our home. This inclusion was not about reciprocating. It was because she was such an integral part of our family and it would never have dawned on us to not include her.

Her life in the church was a work of art. She was an old-line Episcopalian who loved beauty, elegance and tastefulness. But she certainly was not hidebound or unwilling to change. When the new Prayer Book came along, she adopted it without question or debate. After I had been there for four or five years, there was a growing interest among the members in remodeling the interior of the church and making it a little less stark. The job ended up being exquisite. It was Libby who brought the older members along and helped them see the wisdom in the change.

There were a lot of other amazing people in church. One day, a young midwestern fellow by the name of Dave Nalker and his wife, Susie, showed up in church. I had been away recovering from surgery. I came in the back of the church after worship without a clergy shirt on, just to see how things were going in my absence. He ran up to me and treated me as if I were a newcomer, welcoming me to church. Such was my introduction to Dave and Susie. Dave had purchased an International Harvester dealership and he was out to win friends and influence people. A person could not have a better friend and when he became the Senior Warden, he was terrific.

I was involved in the warp and woof of the community. There were two little newspapers. One of them asked me if I would like to write a column. I jumped at the offer. It was called "Cross Purposes," but only occasionally did it carry a religious theme. I would write about people like Mother Harris, who died at 106 but delivered the mail to the other residents of her nursing home right up to her final days, or Claude McLaughlin. One day, eighty-five-year-old Claude and I went up onto Muddy Creek Mountain to see a farmer he knew who sold honey. By the time Claude was finished charming the poor man, we had bought all of his honey for pennies on the dollar. The experience made a great story in my column.

When the *Greenbrier Independent* folded, the only feature the competing paper, the *West Virginia Daily News*, picked up was my weekly column. Altogether, I probably wrote about two hundred pieces.

As a young man, I did what many others did at the time
and smoked cigarettes. Ellen never put one to her lips, which
made her a strong role model for me. Once the evidence about
smoking and lung cancer was developed, I gave up smoking. In
order to stay fit, I began running. It was something of a national
fad at the time. I loved it. Usually, at noon, in lieu of lunch, I
would take off and run six miles. Then, on either Saturday or
Sunday, I would run fifteen or twenty miles. The long runs
could be a challenge as Greenbrier County was mountainous.
I entered a number of races. Just finishing was my goal. The
purpose for my entry was to stay committed to the task. My
favorite races were the fifteen-milers in Charleston. The first
eight miles were all up hill.

After I had been in Lewisburg a few years, I found myself
standing in the middle of Church Street, the street on which we
lived, engaged in a conversation with the executive director of
the Greenbrier Center. As I said earlier, the Greenbrier Center
was a residential facility for mentally challenged youth. This
executive director had asked me to serve on a committee to
ensure that the civil rights of the residents were being honored
and respected. Maybe we were having a conversation about
that work. But somehow, the conversation turned toward other
things. I do not know how the subject of dyslexia came up.
I had never heard that word. I asked him what it was and he
said that it was a kind of "miswiring" of the brain that caused
certain people to have reversal tendencies. I asked him all kinds
of questions about it. I think he thought I was just engaging in
conversation. Then I said in amazement, "It has just dawned
on me that I am dyslexic!" To make sure, he asked me a few
more questions about my situation and then he said, "Yes,

Jim. It sounds like you are. There are varieties and shades
on the dyslexia spectrum and you are on there somewhere."
He then told me something else that proved to be important
to me. He said, "Some of the smartest people you will ever
meet are dyslexic. What dyslexics do is learn to gather and
process information in unique ways. In fact, they learn to solve
problems in ways that no one else ever thinks of. Communities
are enriched when they are welcoming of the unique skills of
dyslexics."

Later on, I learned that one of my, yes, theological heroes,
Albert Einstein, was probably dyslexic. When I think about
Einstein and learning, I am reminded of one of his aphorisms:
"Everyone is a genius. But if you judge a fish by its ability to
climb a tree, it will live its whole life believing that it is stupid."

I felt as if I had been born again. I knew I was not stupid. I
was just different. One of the first things Ellen and I did after
making this discovery was let her become the family chief
financial officer. Back in the '70s, controlling the finances was
usually seen as "men's work." We both knew that she was far
more talented in money management and simple arithmetic
than I could ever be.

Another psychological reality came along at about that time.
I began hanging out with some of the staff of the Greenbrier
Mental Health Clinic. I will say more about that in a little while
but when I was getting to know these people, someone asked
me if I wanted to take a Myers-Briggs test. The Myers-Briggs
test gives the taker an indication of how that person prefers to
live his or her life based on jungian categories. When I took the
test, I learned that I was an *ENFJ*. That is, I was an *E*xtrovert
who was i*N*tuitive, *F*eeling oriented, and *J*udging. It would

take far too long for me to describe all of those concepts, but it was clear to me that this description was accurate. The two middle letters, *N* and *F*, or i*N*tuitive and *F*eeling in my case, stay with you throughout your life. Time and circumstances can influence the outer letters. As I have gotten older, it has become clear to me that I am less *E*xtroverted and increasingly lean toward *I*ntroversion. As it happens, there are times when I operate from one perspective and other times when I operate from the other. I find it a little surprising that only about 15 to 20 percent of the population is *NF*,[24] but the vast majority of Episcopal clergy fit that category. While I used to think I was unique as a clergyman, in fact, I am not.

For the record, Ellen is my exact opposite: she is an *ISTP*. That is, she is an *I*ntrovert who is a *S*ensing, *T*hinking, and *P*erceiving person. As she has matured, she has become more *E*xtroverted. I often say she can get into a conversation with a newel post. In our earlier married years, we did not understand that we were so different and it often produced disagreements. Once we made this discovery, we actually found that it was an enhancement to us as a couple, because, together, we were able to see every issue from just about every direction. I am thankful that she brings balance and perspective to my life.

While the Myers-Briggs test is still highly regarded, a modernized version of the ancient Enneagram has recently gained prominence. I am far less conversant about it, but I do know that I am what they call a three, also known as "the achiever". There are nine different categories. I am told that we are never happy with what we are. I do not like being a three, but I am willing to admit that it is true. A three has,

---

[24] According to Keirsey.com, an online temperament sorter.

so they say, the need to succeed, and a three's top goal is to increase productivity. There is nothing charming about calling yourself a clergyperson and then confessing that your top goal is to increase productivity. It sounds shallow and insincere, but the facts speak for themselves. As Popeye used to say, "I yam what I yam." My entire career as a clergyman was centered on increasing productivity. In the church, it was always about attracting more worshipers, having larger budgets that allowed wider ministries, having a congregation that was more of a leader in the community and making the Episcopal Church more authentically effective. I always expected my sermons and programs to get better. I have worked on this book over and over again because I wanted it to be as authentically mine as I could make it. My vestries usually applauded my actions. Some of my colleagues thought I was misguided and some of the people in the pews thought I was over the top. In fact, I think the Episcopal Church is the most nearly perfect religious institution in the world, and it irritates me to no end that my colleagues are not out there selling the product aggressively. Bishops who do not expect excellence in their clergy give me fits. I think that kind of attitude looks like a three's behavior to me.

One other important experience happened to me while I was in Lewisburg. I had heard about the program at my seminary for clergy who wished to take six weeks away from the parish on a kind of short-term sabbatical to assess their careers and consider their futures. I determined that I could benefit from such a program, so I applied. Up until that time, I had considered myself about a B-level clergyman. I knew I was not bad, but I did not think I was a superstar. With the newfound knowledge that I was not dumb but dyslexic, I began to take another look at who I was and what I could be. During those six weeks, I was led to understand that I was capable of far greater challenges than the ones I had confronted to that point. I began to reconsider how long I would stay in Lewisburg and where I might go. One other joy I received from the course was that I became a friend of the retired headmaster of Choate Rosemary Hall School in Wallingford, Connecticut: Seymour St. John. Choate is one of the finest secondary schools in the world. Just knowing him was an honor. It would be a number of years before my children would be ready for high school, but I understood from Seymour that if they were qualified and wanted that kind of education, he would be glad to help make it happen.

ANNE KATHRYN SELL

Ellen, Andrew, and I were a cozy little family. When Andrew was about five, we would let him walk down Church Street by himself to Washington Street, the main street in town. He would stop off at the corner and go into the gas station to chat with the attendants and buy penny candy. From there, he would walk to Libby Dempsey's office, visit with her for a few minutes and then head back home. Everybody on that end of town knew who he was. Greenbrier County had the lowest crime rate in the state of West Virginia, and West Virginia had the lowest crime rate in America, so we never worried about his well-being. Libby usually called us when he was ready to start back home.

As time marched on, another child seemed like a good idea. Once again, the pregnancy happened quickly once the decision was made. Ellen decided she wanted to see doctors in Roanoke and have the baby there. Andrew wanted a brother he could play with. There was a child on a television show called *3-2-1 Contact* whose name was Hector. Andrew wanted a boy and he wanted him to be named Hector.

When Ellen was due, her doctor suggested that we come down to Roanoke, check into a motel near the hospital and then have the baby the next day. After a pleasant dinner and a good night's sleep near the hospital, we got up bright and early and Ellen checked in. Parents still did not know what the gender of their children would be in advance. They used to use a fetal heart monitor that would give a tentative clue. The indications were that ours was going to be a girl, but we did not know for sure. Had it been a boy, he would have been named William Samuel, because the day of the birth, November 18, 1976, was the seventy-fifth birthday of Ellen's father, William Samuel Major. But, as the doctor suspected, we had a beautiful daughter. My first words to her were "Hello Katie!" She was perfect. At nine pounds nine ounces, she hardly looked like a newborn. We named her Anne Kathryn Sell. Somehow, we did a dirty trick on our children. Without thinking much about it, we ended up calling both of them by their middle names. Much later on in life, Katie would drop the Anne when she became Mrs. Kathryn Sell Garcia.

I drove home that night to tell Andrew. I remember that we were sitting in our bedroom and I said, "Andrew, you now have a little sister. Her name is Katie."

He looked at me with sad eyes and said, "I wanted a brudder." I tried to assuage his disappointment but did not succeed right away. In fact, the next day, I took him to Roanoke to meet his sister. When he met her, he was a properly respectful child. However, he threw up all the way home. I think it was a lot for his little mind to grasp that he was going to be living with a girl. In no time at all, he came to love his sister deeply and joyfully and their childhood together was more than I could ever have hoped for. He was a caring big brother. In fact, when she was older, he took it upon himself to teach her to read.

THE GREENRIER MENTAL HEALTH CLINIC

Ellen had taken a job as an English teacher at Greenbrier East High School. We had a woman who lived close by who was effectively our children's nanny. Her name was Catherine Meredith; we called her Kaki. In the mornings, Andrew and Katie would go to Kaki's house. It was a happy arrangement.

As much as I loved that little church, we struggled to get along financially. I began to cast about for other ways to make money. I do not remember exactly how it happened, but I got into a conversation with Anne Blair Alderson, the Executive Director of the Greenbrier Mental Health Clinic. Parenthetically, if you go back to the genealogical material at the beginning of this memoir, you will see that I was related to the Alderson family. Anne Blair and I were distant cousins, but that had nothing to do with what came next. She initiated a proposal: would I be interested in coming down to the clinic from four to six in the afternoon to see clients who might otherwise be unable to get there because of their work schedules. She made it clear that I would be supervised and that my supervisor would be available for support and consultation. I was pleased. It was exactly the kind of supplemental job I had been looking for. It did not conflict with my church responsibilities. I knew the staff. They knew me. It was an easy transition.

On the staff was a young social worker named Greg
Johnson. A transplant from Florida, he had found his way to
West Virginia University, where he had earned a Master's in
Social Work (MSW). He was not quite an earthal, but he lived
out in the country, wore plaid work shirts and jeans, and made
his own granola. He ended up living in a log cabin. Maybe he
was kind of a hybrid earthal. In other words, he kind of looked
the part of an earthal, but was pretty main stream in much of
his lifestyle. We took to each other right away. He had just
started dating a young schoolteacher and potter from Alderson
named Libby Meadows. She was the perfect partner for him.
Greg went on many years later to write his own delightful
memoir and his courtship and marriage to Libby Meadows
were featured.[25]

Greg had been raised a Roman Catholic, and Libby was a
Presbyterian. To split the difference, they became Episcopalians
and joined St. James. How great was that? I now had good
friends and professional colleagues who were also members of
the church. Greg and I took on many projects together. If you
read his memoir, look for the character called Father Andy.
It is a thinly disguised Jim Sell. He tells some pretty funny
stories about our exploits. One particularly pleasant but serious
activity we enjoyed was giving a paper together at the National
Association of Rural Social Workers in Laramie, Wyoming.
Ellen, Andrew, and I flew out there with Greg and Libby; we
had a fine time giving the paper and seeing some of the West.
I remember little Andrew actually playing in the snow in the
Snowy Range on the Fourth of July.

---

[25] Greg Johnson, *A Very Famous Social Worker,* IUniverse Press:
Bloomington IN (2011).

AFTER NEARLY 100 YEARS ...

After an initial few years in Lewisburg, I began to concoct a plan to unite all the Episcopal churches in the county. There were four of them. There was never any intention to actually merge them. A loose confederation seemed like the best solution. We called ourselves the Greenbrier Parish. Basically, this arrangement came into existence and functioned for five years. In that time, several clergy colleagues came along to work with me. Birk Stathers was the one I was closest to. His wife, Molly, and I went to South Hills Country Day School together right after World War II. If you have not figured this out already, let me just say that West Virginia is a small place and people are interconnected on many levels.

Under this parish arrangement, I would take services in Lewisburg and Ronceverte one Sunday while Birk took services in the two White Sulphur Springs churches. Then, the next Sunday, we would switch.

During this time, we had one other connection to life in White Sulphur. While Ellen taught for most of her time there, for a while, she also worked in Peck's, the women's shop at the Greenbrier. That job was a change of pace for her and for us. It allowed us to see some of that incredible hotel up close and personal for a few years.

Regardless of the confederation of churches, St. James grew the fastest and strongest. In 1977, it became a self-supporting, fully independent parish in the Diocese of West Virginia. After nearly one hundred years as a mission, it was free to call its own Rector and I was elected. (Despite humorous threats to the contrary, no one else was nominated.)[26]

WHAT I REALLY LEARNED IN LEWISBURG

This is going to sound naive because it is naive, but back when I first thought about going into the ordained ministry, I had a vision of life in the church that is almost laughable. I thought the position was going to be boringly quaint. A friend of Ellen's mother gave us a book entitled something like *How to Marry a Minister* (of course, we were already married). It was depressing. As we read it, we assumed that the author wanted her readers to know that if all other prospects failed and marriage was the chief goal in the life of a young lady, a pickle-faced man in a black shirt might still be snagged. Her life would be tedious but not lived out alone.

Earlier, when we were married, the wife of the Dean of VTS gave Ellen and me two books for gifts. One provided tips for planting a vegetable garden and the other was about canning and freezing vegetables. (Actually, they came in handy in Lewisburg.) I could see my life unfolding in the most stiflingly quaint way. I would live in a monotonous world, surrounded by sweetly dull people, while I tended my glebe lands,[27] planting my garden and canning my vegetables. The words of the Beatles' "Eleanor Rigby" would probably come to pass: "Father McKinsey, wiping the dirt from his hands as

---

[26] The title of the clergyperson in a self-supporting parish is called the Rector. A Vicar is in charge of a mission under the direct supervision of the Bishop.

[27] In Colonial America, land would be set apart for the use of the rector of the church. It was called glebe land.

he walked from the grave. No one was saved...all the lonely people." But here is the irony. It was the lonely people who saved me from a life of professional alienation and frustration.

Something happened that I later came to realize is part of the day-in, day-out routine of a parish clergyperson. People were hungry to share their lives with me. People who saw no other credentials than three uncompelling years of church history, Bible studies, and theology would tell me the deepest secrets about themselves. The reasons were manifold. Some told me stories to see if they could shock me. Other secrets came from people who simply did not have any other person to talk to. A few were deeply confessional. I heard about abuse, scandal, crime and failure. I heard from sociopaths and the profoundly mentally ill. I heard from conspiracy theorists, deviants, and the dispossessed. I heard from mystics, spiritualists, and the born again. But mostly, I heard from plain ole Episcopalians who came to church, said their prayers and tried to get along in life. And most of them seemed to have one deep-seated agenda. To one degree or another, they yearned to know about the acceptability of their very souls. They wanted some small shred of hope that they were not so bad, perverse, mean, or despicable that they could not be loved by God. The irony in all of this is that many of these people were simply incapable of changing very much. They did not know how to turn their lives around. Even those who remained unattractive people, maybe even bad people, still hoped for salvation.

I remember Otis. That was not his real name, but he was real. Otis was awful. No one could have liked Otis. Think of the banker in *It's a Wonderful Life* - the guy played by Lionel Barrymore. That was Otis. There was nothing about Otis that

I found attractive. Yet even he knew what a jerk he was, and contradiction of contradictions, despite his unwillingness or inability to turn his life around and make amends, his deepest prayer was to be deemed worthy.

As the first decade of my life in the ordained ministry unfolded, I discovered that there was nothing tedious or quaint about what I was in the midst of. This could not be a monotonous life if a person kept his defenses down and was willing to listen without accusing. My job was not to call balls and strikes. Compassion trumped judgment every time. Every person was important and every story was of God - true, profound and captivating.

WHO IS SAVED?

As the years unfolded and I had new chapters added to my career, I discovered that what applied to the few applied to the many. Behind the carefully constructed persona of every parishioner was a man or woman with a deeply powerful, personal and, perhaps, painful story to tell. I saw that the failures, inadequacies and insufficiencies of many people had the capacity to beat them down. Somehow, most of them managed to cobble together existences that came across as heroic to me. Each had found a way to get up out of bed in the morning and face yet one more onslaught from reality. They suffered ample experiences of hell in this life without necessarily having to relive them all over again in eternity. It was during this time that I made the wager of my soul and began preaching universal salvation. If it turns out that I have been preaching a lie, then I will lose the wager and God will have to chastise me for my arrogance. I believe that God exists,

God is the author of creation, and God is love. Therefore, God does not dismiss his beloved creatures just because they are too caught up in their own self-centeredness to see that abiding love which is the first fruits of eternal heaven right here and now. Not to discover God's love is to miss out on a great earthly joy, but God forgives our shortcomings in the final analysis.

As I said at the beginning of this chapter, the people of Lewisburg taught me far more than I ever could have dreamed of.

CHAPTER 4

LEARNING TO BELIEVE

I cannot begin to put a date on the time when I could finally
stand in front of the mirror and tell myself in total honesty that
I was a believing Christian. There are at least two ways for a
person to be spiritually transformed. The one that gets the most
publicity is the "Amazing Grace" variety. The author of that
great hymn, John Newton, an Englishman who was a sailor
and slave trader, was in a horrible storm at sea. The ship was
sinking. When he cried out to God for salvation, some of the
cargo shifted around and plugged a hole in the sinking ship. He
and the ship survived. After that experience, he wrote "Amazing
Grace," wherein he said, "I once was lost but now am found,
was blind, but now I see." It was a celebration of his rejection
of slavery, his physical rescue, and his spiritual transformation,
all at the same time. People who have these experiences have
intriguing stories to tell. Only the most narrow-minded skeptic
would doubt at least the possible legitimacy of such an event.
It is as if people like Newton are thrown on top of a hot grill,
get basted by the Holy Spirit and are quickly roasted until they
are well done.

Then there are people like me. I was not basted. I was
marinated in a slowly penetrating sauce and then allowed to

stew in my own juices for a long period of time over a low heat rotisserie. But what works is what matters. During my early years in the ministry, there was a broadly based renewal of spirituality in all denominations, including the Episcopal Church, called the charismatic movement. People's new life of faith was celebrated in all kinds of experiences that were evidence of the power of the Holy Spirit. The litmus test of the charismatic movement was the gift of speaking in tongues, or glossolalia. The Bible defines such a phenomenon as being endowed with a spiritual gift of a universal language that is understandable to the faithful people who are present. I am from West Virginia. When I was a high school boy, some friends of mine and I slipped into a snake-handling church (and slipped right back out when the snakes appeared!). I had had my fill of speaking in tongues, snake handling, instantaneous healing, and all kinds of unsubstantiated claims of the rural fundamentalist culture. I had known of churches that did not have an organ because organs were not mentioned in the Bible and women who shortened their hair by beating it between two rocks because scissors were not in the Bible either. As far as I was concerned, there was no perceptible difference between the modern charismatic movement and backwoods camp meeting revivalism. I was going to be a tough nut to crack.

Somewhere along the way, I made an intellectual decision. I decided that there were about six or seven arenas of the human experience that I needed to develop if I hoped to have an abundant life. I would argue that they can be a workable list of core fundamentals for living all persons everywhere can consider. We need to find and express authentic human love so that we can be emotionally healthy. As a subset to that, we need to strive for compassion because respecting the dignity of every human being brings peace and justice. We need to stretch ourselves educationally because our minds are the greatest gifts of our lives and require our enhancements. We need to exercise our bodies and not eat and drink foolishly in order to care for what we are physically. If we bring children into the world, we need to support and love them unstintingly because they are our blessing and joy. We need to work hard at jobs or careers to be productive members of the human community and because our work gives us an identity and reason to live. Most importantly, we need to be attentive to our souls, whatever they are, because there is clearly some connection between our innate self-worth and that deep down universal spark of the divine we call life.

So my spiritual quest began as part of a self-improvement quest. The first questions for me were the following: Was I capable of believing in God, and who did I think God was? Actually, some of coming to terms with the reality of God was pretty manageable. I said earlier that I had had two profound experiences that were both beyond cognition but not hallucinatory. God was out there somewhere and I knew it. Who is God? We are living in the golden age of astronomy and physics and I have been a long time lay student of those fields. On one end of the physical spectrum, the universe is so phenomenal and orderly that only a fool would call it an accident. On the other end, an exploration of neutrons and quarks leads especially wise and enlightened people to the conclusion that "In the beginning, God created the heavens and the earth."[28] The sound of the Big Bang is the ongoing echo of the creation by God. The Higgs boson is an element that

---

[28] This is the first verse of Genesis.

brings order out of chaos. To me, God is the prime mover of the heavens and the earth, the life force that generates something out of nothing and the abiding source of love that ties all things, animate and inanimate, together.

Then I had to grapple with the harder stuff. I was willing and prepared to accept as true much of the historical data. The claims about Pontius Pilate and the crucifixion were not the subject of doubt. It was what Christianity claimed about Mary and Jesus that caused me to wonder. The incarnation and resurrection are the heart of the matter. It all had to be intellectually honest and spiritually captivating, or I knew I would have to live the life of quiet desperation of a frustrated little fraud, because I was not going to buy it otherwise. But slowly, over the years, I began opening myself to new and intriguing perspectives. A number of authors were important for me.

First, there were the authors of Genesis. If you had been living maybe 2,500 years ago and someone asked you what you knew about the beginnings of time and history, in all likelihood, you would have recounted the mythologies of your ancestors. Real myths are not obsessed with getting the facts right. They rise to a higher level. Early on, perhaps there was some expectation that they were literally true, but facts keep like fish. Anyone who gets weighed down by too many facts is in trouble, no matter what the subject or historical context is. As soon as we think one set of facts is true, new information comes along that either edits or voids it. The sages who wrote that document had a greater sermon to preach than the stories of God creating the heavens and the earth in seven days or Abraham journeying to distant lands. The real message was that God acts in history and history is moving in a particular direction. When one looks back over the span of history, it is easy to conclude that God was involved in the past and, therefore, continues to be involved today. Despite the fact that we do all we can to violate God's world and destroy God's people, Jesus, in his classic Lord's Prayer, said that God's ultimate realm is coming and that God's ultimate will is being done. Einstein once said, "That which is impenetrable to us really exists. Behind the secrets of nature remains something subtle, intangible, and inexplicable. Veneration for this force beyond anything that we can comprehend is my religion." In a related way, in his best-selling book, *A Brief History of Time*, physicist Stephen Hawking claimed that when physicists find the theory he and his colleagues are looking for – his "unified theory" - then they will have seen into "the mind of God". Those both sound a lot like both Genesis to me.

The next author was the man who wrote the Gospel according to St. John. No wonder the fundamentalists and evangelicals do not know what to do with this writer. He came along thirty or forty years after Matthew, Mark, and Luke and did not care about facts or details. He could not even get the timeline right. He knew nothing about a virgin birth, magi, or stars in the east. Those things were not important to him. Yes, he talked about Jesus and his death and resurrection. Everything he reported was in the form of poetry and metaphor. It all has multiple meanings. Under the literal narrative, there is a proclamation that Jesus is the Christ, the Messiah, the man who is full of the power of God. At his most basic level, John is saying that if a person considers the claim that Jesus is able to describe God and God's will accurately and if he or she makes some attempt to live a life that is consistent with that claim, that person will experience a taste and a touch of what it truly means to be human. We are all part of God's creation, so God is revealed in each of us. What makes Jesus the special Son of God is that we get a far better view of God through him than through other people. To me, the symbolic imagery of St. John does a far better job of pointing to God in the man Jesus than many of the stories of Matthew, Mark and Luke. Those reporters caused us to be in endless arguments these past two thousand years. John understood that any attempt to describe Jesus in plainspoken prose would simply fall short because it would be encased in human terms that unavoidably narrow our perspective.

Then there was the remarkable St. Patrick from fifth century Celtic Ireland. The first thing to know about him is that Ireland was the only place on Earth that was evangelized without a drop of blood being spilled. Everywhere else, overly zealous missionaries made people offers they could not refuse. They could either be baptized or be killed. The choice was that simple. But this Englishman, Patrick, loved the unruly Irish into the church. He was not exclusive about whom he welcomed. As one who made friends among the terrifying Irish army, he welcomed soldiers of all ranks and backgrounds, as well as noblewomen and prostitutes. Those from other faiths, such as the Druids, were honored for their traditions and welcomed in ways they found compatible. Patrick was sort of a contemporary of St. Augustine of Hippo, but it is almost as if the two men were of different religions. We have an exquisite writing of St. Patrick known as St. Patrick's Breastplate.[29] Oh my heavens! It is my true creed! It is a poem to the expansiveness of God's

---

[29] For the text, see appendix 1.

love and compassion. Maybe the self-absorbed religious fringe would call it un-Christian because it carries with it a kind of Eastern pantheism, but in truth, it soars far beyond the confines of ancient orthodoxies. It fits well into the perspectives of the modern creation spiritualists, such as Matthew Fox and Pierre Teilhard de Chardin. I could go on forever about this wondrous man, but in summary, I will say that my soul dwells in the unique Celtic spirituality of St. Patrick and his colleagues.

There are a couple of lesser known individuals whom I might lump together into what I would call the heart of the Anglican consciousness. Dame Julian of Norwich, a somewhat strange fifteenth century English nun, was accused by the church hierarchy of being a proto-universalist. That clearly makes her my kind of woman! For Julian, suffering was not a punishment that God inflicted, as was the common understanding at the time. She believed that God loved everyone and wanted to save them all. Her most famous quote to make this point was "All shall be well and all shall be well and all manner of thing shall be well."[30] She also thought, as Patrick did, that the greatest miracle of all was the lives we were living. She would hold out a hazelnut and proclaim that all of the created universe could be reduced to the miracle within it. It began with new life and continued to renew itself with the eternal seed within the seed. Again, she is worth spending more time on, but I will stop here.

The other quiet little superstar in my galaxy is Richard Hooker, who died in 1600. He found himself caught between Calvinists on one side and the Roman Catholics on the other. He wanted to state a claim that Anglicans dwelled decidedly

---

[30] A phrase picked up by T. S. Eliot in his poem "Little Gedding," from *Four Quartets* (1942).

between those two polarities. While he did not specifically come up with the term *via media*, or middle way, that is the position he staked out for Anglicanism. He encouraged us to be the moderate, well-grounded faith that avoided the pitfalls of the extremists. He also invited us to operate from a "three legged stool" of scripture, tradition, and reason. The Calvinists (think Presbyterians and Baptists) love scripture. The Catholics love tradition. We combine them both and add the seasoning of intelligent evaluation of the issues before us. I think that if worldwide Christianity took such a perspective seriously, we would suffer from less polarization and hypocrisy.

Then there are the modern writers. I was trained with a healthy infusion of classic contemporary theologians, especially the big three: Paul Tillich, Karl Barth, and Reinhold Niebuhr. Although they were decidedly different, these were the leaders of what was called the Neo-orthodox movement of twentieth century Christianity. They were beyond brilliant, but a problem for me. It seemed as if they kept their heads in philosophical clouds when I needed well-grounded examples of spiritual connectivity. Then they all died and no one came along to replace them. Their deaths were the end of an era and for a long time, the intellectually rich theological ship that is so necessary for wise judgment was rudderless. Slowly, a different category of spiritual thinker evolved. Some of them dove right into the center of my concerns because they spoke of real life problems that people like me faced.

Frederick Buechner authored novels, personal memoirs, and books on the spiritual life. I have read most of his memoirs and contemplative writings. His style of writing and his method of articulating personal faith changed me forever. In my earlier years of preaching, I probably sought to pattern myself after John Harper of St. John's, Lafayette Square, who was erudite and sophisticated but not self-revealing. That worked. I wanted to protect myself while I struggled with my own journey. Buechner is a storyteller. Many of the stories he tells are ones from his own experience. They are fraught with pain confronting hope, possibility in the face of meaninglessness, and death overcome by resurrection. From Buechner, I discovered that a well told story is a universal story. I have become a storyteller. My story will never be your story, but if I share it honestly and carefully, as I am trying to do in this book, you can pick through it and discover something true for yourself. All my preaching in the last thirty years has been an attempt to preach like Frederick Buechner writes.[31]

Joseph Campbell, a professor at Sarah Lawrence College, was an autodidact who never graduated from college. I first became aware of him when he did an eight-part PBS series of interviews with Bill Moyers. Some of the glow seems to have diminished from Campbell's star in recent years, but he did provide a perspective that I think I knew all along. I just needed someone to spell it out. His most popular books, such as *The Power of Myth* and *The Hero's Journey*, look at how certain myths and archetypal stories seem to reappear in many different cultures and societies. For example, the Jewish creation myth and flood in Genesis have their parallels in other ancient stories around the world. There are a series of medieval philosophical arguments for the existence of God

---

[31] It is an honor for me that my daughter, Katie, elected to attend the Lawrenceville School in Lawrenceville, New Jersey. It is also Buechner's alma mater and where he taught many years ago as a young man.

called ontological arguments. Basically, they claim that human beings are incapable of having a conception of God unless there is something real that gives rise to that conception. There are flaws that smart logicians can find in arguments like that, but I think some of Joseph Campbell's notion about archetypal mythology resides here. Perhaps our minds are hardwired to believe in divine things because divine things exist. One of Campbell's myths, the hero's journey, sounds a lot like Jesus, with his death and resurrection. But in fact, it is a myth that echoes in a number of other places and times.

To me, there is something self-validating about ancient religions. Specifically, the great Abrahamic faiths of Judaism, Christianity and Islam, the eastern saga of Hinduism and Buddhism, Native American religion, Norse and Germanic mythology, and African and pre-Christian Celtic spirituality all would not have entered the consciousness of humans if there were not some underlying causality. These were independently developed faiths that had their genesis in some kind of primary revelations. In other words, there is something out there that gives substance to the faith of us all. Because of my geography, history and cultural experience, I fell onto one particular facet of that divine gemstone we call Christianity and it fits my worldview comfortably.

The great dividing line between who I was and what I am is the Rt. Rev. John Shelby Spong. I first heard about Jack when I was in seminary. He was already causing the Episcopal Church to sit up and take notice. Born and raised in Charlotte, North Carolina, Jack attended the University of North Carolina and the Virginia Theological Seminary. Eventually, he ended up as the Rector of St. Paul's Episcopal Church in Richmond. At that

time, Jack began his literary life. He wrote several books in
Richmond. In 1979, he was elected the Bishop of the Diocese
of Newark, New Jersey. Once he was in Newark, he became
a prolific author. I think he is up to about twenty-four books.
I have read almost all of them. I think he has been a primary
proponent for most of the priorities and standards we have
today in the Episcopal Church. Our church's memory of him
will last a long time, because he foresaw what we could become
and gave energy to his vision. He himself will say that religion
is a mixed blessing. I concur. There are times when I love it and
sometimes I scratch my head in confusion. But Jack has kept
me holding onto the might and majesty of the church.

Well into his episcopacy, he became the most articulate
spokesperson for the great issues confronting the Episcopal
Church: women's ordination, gay and lesbian ordination, the
consecration of gay and lesbian bishops, and marriage equality
for the LGBT community. A point of personal pride for me is
that one of his books, *Living In Sin*, a treatise on some of these
pivotal issues, is dedicated to several of my colleagues and me.

So how do I answer the question "What do I believe?" Or
how do I score myself on, say, the Apostles' Creed? I think I give
myself an A. Do not be confused. I believe it metaphorically,
poetically, and spiritually. Do I believe in the virgin birth?
Other than the fact that it is metaphorically rich, I cannot see
any reason why I should bother? It is so far removed from what
I think is important that I consider it irrelevant and immaterial.
As I said, St. John never even mentioned it. In fact, he never
mentioned a lot of things, such as miracles. He did suggest
that there were certain remarkable occasions when "signs of
the coming of God's kingdom" were offered for interpretation.

He spoke in images that go beyond language and faith. They transcend time and space, as did St. Patrick, Dame Julian and many others.

I have not spoken of the biggest sign or miracle on the table, the one matter that finally separates Christianity from all other religions: the resurrection of Jesus Christ. I have two beliefs about the resurrection. The first one is that I do think something unique, extraordinary and beyond time and space happened on that first Easter morning. It forever remains a mystery to everyone exactly what happened. I think that the power of the event lies in the mystery. We will never have an objective, clinical, cognitive explanation. But whatever happened that morning changed history dramatically. Right up to the present day, the resurrection of Jesus Christ resonates through history and continues to turn heads around for a new look at it. I believe Christianity would have never survived the Enlightenment and our contemporary scientific world had it all been based on a fraud. Someone would have figured it out and it would have been dismissed out of hand. Nothing like that has ever happened.

The other belief I have regarding the resurrection is this: I think it brought a new way of living into the human experience. From Easter Day forward, whether we are people of the Christian tradition or not, we have bought into a certain kind of backdoor faith. We have taken it as fundamentally true that hope wins out over the worst possible destruction. For every sickness, there can be healing. After every darkness, there is a dawn. For every failure, there can be a new possibility. When one door closes, another can open. Despite the pain and suffering that swirls around us, Western Civilization does not believe in complete hopelessness. Other than the most pessimistic or wounded, most of us believe that hope abides and a better life awaits. There is a straight line connecting that faith with the first Easter Day.

And what about our own personal resurrections? Are you and I going to some heaven of eternal bliss? Believing that we will is clearly the best choice among all the possible alternatives, but just like what will happen five minutes from now, it is a mystery. We do not know what the future holds, but we usually remain positively expectant. Whatever happens at our deaths takes place well outside of the categories of time and space that have been our operating norms since the Big Bang. The day I stopped having panic attacks was the same day I stopped worrying about my personal resurrection. I am as curious as you are, but I am content to let the process unfold the same way I let the upcoming hour reveal itself when it comes.

When we treat the Christian faith as one arm of God's revelation in history and not as a club to hammer on those who disagree with us, we begin to place ourselves in a far holier context. When we use our moral leverage to enable others to live abundant lives filled with faith, peace and love, we are doing God's work. The greatest sentence to be uttered in the second millennium was from Martin Luther before the Diet of Worms. Told that he must obey the church and its teachings, he demurred. He said, "Here I stand. I cannot do otherwise. God help me. Amen." He was not going to be told what he must believe and how he must act. He would rely on his own personal value system with its internal faith experience and let the chips fall where they may. Thus began the liberation of ideas and peoples from the tyranny of the state and the church.

All of the battles that my generation has engaged in from civil rights through marriage rights had their beginnings in Martin Luther's courage. The church does have the capacity to change the world, but only when it elevates people's visions of life and argues for authenticity in all things. Either God is big enough to act in history, as Genesis explains, or we are entrapped in a closed universe defined by self-aggrandizing spiritual tyrants. And they will end up causing us to lose the whole shebang, the wonderful church of Jesus Christ.

CHAPTER 5

STEPPING INTO THE WORLD

What you need to understand at this juncture is that with the exception of my sister, the most direct lines of my family had been residents of West Virginia for generations. My parents were so tied to their home that when Ellen and I began suggesting that we might consider moving to another state, the announcement put my mother into a dither. She told us endless stories of people who had left West Virginia for what they had thought would be greener pastures, only to be broken by the experience. My mother was pretty sure that we would be stepping beyond our comfort level. But what she failed to understand was that I was married to a woman who had had a wide range of experiences in other states and other countries. Ellen knew that "the only thing we had to fear was fear itself."[32] It was time to leave. If there was any chance I might get cold feet, I was lovingly pushed out the door by the bold, adventuresome Ellen.

I do not remember how much money I was making when I left Lewisburg in 1980, but it was well below the national average for Episcopal clergy with my experience, even with the little supplement I received as a counselor at the Greenbrier

---

[32] A reference from FDR's first inaugural address.

Mental Health Clinic. Katie was three and Andrew was eight. Ellen and I could take a long range view and see that there was no way that we could afford to give them a first class education if both she and I did not improve our financial lot.

I began to cast my net, looking around to see if there was another part of the world into which we might be able to make a comfortable transition. It was not easy. As I said earlier, the fact that I had served in three small communities over a period of about ten years did not look great on my résumé. I had plenty of successes that I could claim, but self-promotion made me uncomfortable. I used to wish that I had an agent, as professional athletes did, who could be my intermediary. Of course, there were no such people and I was left to my own devices.

In 1979, I went back to VTS for my tenth class reunion. My friend and classmate Leslie Smith had just been called to the church in Bloomfield/Glen Ridge, New Jersey, in the Diocese of Newark. He arrived there after having a long and successful tenure as Associate Rector of the Church of the Epiphany in Washington, D.C. Those were impressive credentials for a young clergyman. I had no such equal qualifications. As we talked, I said, "I would like to live in the Diocese of Newark, but I do not have a way to get a foot in the door."

"You have me, don't you?" Leslie said.

"Yes, but you are brand new there, and you do not have any clout," I said.

"Oh yes I do," he said. He then told me something that I thought was fascinating: whenever a new clergyperson came into the Diocese of Newark, the Bishop, Jack Spong, would ask him or her to come up with a couple of names of competent clergypersons who might be interested in leaving their current position. Jack Spong spoiled me on so many levels as a bishop. Not only was he a visionary and prophet, but he was also the shrewdest manager I ever saw in the episcopacy. To this day, I have not known of another bishop who proactively recruited clergy like he did. As we departed, Leslie said, "I will give Jack your name. Do not worry. Something will come of this."

I was appreciative but dubious. I had had two or three churches take a look at me and turn me down. None of them were in what I would call highly selective places. There was no reason for me to think the next prospective church would be any different. But a month or two passed, and one day, I was sitting in my office in Lewisburg when the phone rang. "Hello?" I said.

The voice on the other end of the line said, "Is this Jim Sell?"

"Yes."

"This is Jack Spong, calling from the Diocese of Newark. Leslie Smith tells me you might be a person we might encourage to come to our diocese. Is that true?"

I could not believe it. This was not Jim Sell standing, hat in hand, hoping someone would notice him in the crowd. This was the world-famous John Shelby Spong recruiting me. He was not having one of his deployment staff make the call. He was reaching down into the hills of West Virginia himself and treating me as if I really mattered to him. I was thrilled. I would have taken any church he threw my way, but he was far more appropriate than that. He said, "We have several possibilities developing. Could you write me a letter describing the kind of church you would be most interested in? I will then look around and see how we can proceed."

Oh my goodness, I thought. What had Leslie told him about me? Had he overblown my abilities? Were my mother's fears going to come true? Was I about to rise to my level of incompetence? Would I go to sophisticated New Jersey only to fail like a whipped dog and have to come back to West Virginia to spend the rest of my life in Avondale hollow?

When I went home and told Ellen, she was a little skeptical. Most of what we knew about northern New Jersey was the string of towns along the New Jersey Turnpike and the Garden State Parkway. Her oft-recollected response was "Where are we going? Bayonne?" (Actually, Bayonne has its charms!) Making the right move was important to us. We knew that these would be the transitional years of our family life. I was becoming a little less optimistic when I wrote Jack and said that he needed to understand that I had two small-town children who would never be comfortable in the hustle and bustle of an urban or fast-paced suburban community. While we might prefer something away from the maddening crowds, we were at a point in time when the quality of the public school education was important to us.

SPARTA, NEW JERSEY

I about fell over a few weeks later when Jack Lynch, the Senior Warden of St. Mary's Church in Sparta, called me. He said that they were looking for a new rector and that Bishop Spong had recommended me. If I had designed the perfect parish for me at that stage in my career and the perfect residential community for my family, it would have looked exactly like St. Mary's. Sparta is located in the northwest of New Jersey, in Sussex County. When we arrived there, there were about fifteen thousand residents in the township. The rumor was that there were more cattle than people in Sussex County. That was never confirmed, but it seemed to have a kind of rural charm that felt comfortable to us. Within the township was Lake Mohawk. It was built in the 1920s and '30s as a summer refuge for New Yorkers and urban-oriented New Jersey families. What had started with rustic vacation cottages around a lovely man-made mountain lake had morphed into comfortable year-round homes.

Sparta was a classic bedroom community. There was no industry and little commerce. The southern border of the township edged up against more developed Morris County. Most people commuted, as they said, "down below," to one of the other northern New Jersey counties to work. Two buses a day delivered those who worked in New York City to the Port Authority bus terminal in the morning and back home at night. When I came back from my first trip up there and told Ellen that there was no walk-along type Main Street, she did not know what to make of that. The social life of the community centered on two interests: the churches and the many sports programs for youth. A uniqueness of Sparta was that it was a town heavily populated by commercial airline pilots and other flight personnel. At the time, New Jersey did not have a state income tax, so many pilots moved to Sparta rather than New York or Connecticut because they could save money while they enjoyed the abundant recreational amenities during their time off. This was before the time of discount airlines and the pilots' union established generous rules for their employees. Full captains working for an international airline like Pan Am or TWA lived as well as a successful doctor or lawyer and were in the air fewer than one hundred hours a month. They thought nothing of deadheading (catching a free lift on any airline) to some distant airport to pick up the flight they had been assigned. Commuting to Newark, LaGuardia, or even JFK airport was not a burden. In their extended off hours, they could enjoy spending time at the lake in the summer and skiing a little farther north in Sussex County in the winter.

I had two interviews at St. Mary's. The first time, I flew there by myself. I was picked up at the airport by the wife of the Senior Warden, Carol Lynch. By the time we arrived at their home, she had sold me on the church. All I could think was, *If this congregation is made up of people like Carol, I am packing my bags and coming as soon as possible.* Almost no one living in Sparta was a native. Carol and Jack were both from Louisville, Kentucky. Carol was a homemaker and mother of five. Jack was a successful businessman. They both had their feet on the ground and a deep commitment to the life and ministry of their church. I am most comfortable when I am around people with a moderate, accepting view of the world, tempered by a faithfulness that is usually seen rather than heard. This was what I saw first in Carol and later when I met Jack.

The interviews and introductions went well. There was one particular moment that I especially remember. Jack said that he wanted me to meet the parish treasurer. His name was Henry Richardson. Since he was getting along in years, it was hard for him to get out much, so we went by his home to visit for a few moments. Henry was a charming, old-school English gentleman. He had been a highly successful Certified Public Accountant, with his own firm in Passaic. At one point, he and his wife, Frances, had bought a vacation home in Sparta, where they and their children had come in the summers. After his retirement, they had moved there permanently. I sat on the sofa beside Frances. She and I were having a convivial conversation about life in the town and church. I then asked her how many children she had. She looked at me with a quizzical look and said, "Oh, two or three, I think. I am not exactly sure."

I regained my composure instantly. There had been no indication that she might be suffering from the early stages of Alzheimer's disease, but I got it. Henry gave a wry smile as if to say, "Thank you, Jim, for understanding," and gently answered the question himself: three.

Henry and I ended up having a wonderful relationship. In fact, his older son, Bill Richardson, who became the President of Johns Hopkins University and, later, the head of the enormous W. K. Kellogg Foundation, became a great family friend. Between my old friend Seymour St. John and Bill, a highly esteemed alumnus of Choate Rosemary Hall School, my children's ultimate acceptance to that stunning institution, the alma mater of John F. Kennedy and Adlai E. Stevenson Jr., was increasingly enhanced.

The vestry seemed to feel positively disposed toward me and I liked them immensely. I went home to report the news to Ellen. She was cautiously pleased but not sold. At that point, no one had offered me a job. But within a few days, Jack Lynch called and asked if I could return with Ellen for another round of conversations. As I recall, they were down to two candidates. Ellen had her agenda, which was important. While she was interested in seeing the rectory and the neighborhood in which we would live, she was vitally interested in Helen Morgan School, the neighborhood elementary school.

This time, we stayed at the home of the Junior Warden, Fred Noble and his wife, Mickey. Fred was an engineer and tinkerer who had designed a device for sharpening high quality drill bits. Mickey was his perpetually smiling, winsome spouse. They were both extroverts who displayed all the charm of classic New Jersey culture. Fred was determined to have me called to the church. Unbeknownst to me, he and Mickey pulled an end run on the whole search process. The night we were there, he said, "We have a wonderful community theater called the Cornerstone Theater. Tonight they are putting on the classic Cole Porter musical comedy *Anything Goes*. I will get tickets."

What I did not understand was that he knew that about half of the St. Mary's congregation would be in the audience. Fred and Mickey escorted Ellen and me around to everyone and introduced me as a prospective candidate. Henry Richardson told me later that he sat there and watched me from afar to see if I had a sense of humor. He did not want some stuffed-shirt clergyperson and that was his way of evaluating my personality. When it was all over with, the other candidate did not have a fair chance. The buzz through the congregation was that Jim Sell was the right person to come to St. Mary's.

The next day, Ellen and I had an appointment with the principal of Helen Morgan School. We could tell that the school ran by the highest professional standards and that the quality of the education was without question.

On Palm Sunday afternoon in 1980, I received a call from Jack Lynch, inviting me to become only the second Rector of St. Mary's Church, Sparta. All of the Sell family hearts were broken at the prospect of leaving our beloved Lewisburg, but the time had come for us to spread our wings and this was the right place to begin our flight.

We thought we were doing the right thing by leaving Lewisburg as soon as possible and relocating to Sparta in the spring. We arrived in early May so that Andrew would have about six weeks to get to know some of his classmates before the long, lonely summer. Unfortunately, that was not a good move. As it was near the end of the school year, the other second graders had been together for over eight months and the likelihood that they would incorporate somebody new was not great. It did not happen. Fortunately, he had his little sister whom he adored and who loved being with him. We joined the local community pool and Ellen worked hard to find fun things for them to do. Together, they muddled through the spring and summer, hoping a new school year would bring happier results. Katie attended a day camp at nearby Engle School. At three, she was young enough to be able to fit easily into her peer group. Andrew tried to connect with some of the neighborhood children, but he did not find his place until sweet Lloyd and Wendy Tillman moved in across the street a few months later. They were new too and grateful to find Andrew waiting for them.

One of the special joys I had was to be the official parent who stood with Katie when she was picked up by the school bus for kindergarten and who was there when she was dropped off in the afternoon. I did it for several years, well into primary school. There was a sizable rock on the edge of the yard where Katie would sit waiting for the bus. For years, that was known as "Katie's rock."

As I said, every move we ever made wreaked havoc on Ellen. I would come into a new parish and be surrounded by people who were happy to meet me. This was certainly true in Sparta. Everywhere I turned, people made me feel welcome. It was Ellen who had to worry about all the day-to-day activities of community life. Not only did the matter of our children's well-being fall to her, but she also had to negotiate finding doctors, dentists, grocery stores, and all the other basics of living. Then she needed to look for a job. While she was always successful, it was just one more stress she had to endure. All the while, she was missing her old friends and familiar surroundings in Lewisburg. I swore to myself that I would never put her through this kind of dislocation again. She did not like it and I understood why. It was a promise I did not keep, as we moved to Virginia ten years later.

St. Mary's Church

St. Mary's had a curious history. After World War I, a young army veteran fresh out of the General Theological Seminary had arrived in Sparta to begin the Western Episcopal Mission of New Jersey. Sparta was up in the mountains, rural and without any churches. The Rev. Edwin Ford, their new Vicar, was probably not the kind of person one would have expected among these country people. A direct descendent of a famous Morristown family noted for loaning George Washington their home during the Revolutionary War, Ford was an aristocratic gentleman with deep Anglo-Catholic credentials.[33] He insisted upon being called Father Ford. Being an independently wealthy

---

[33] *Anglo-Catholicism* is a term that used to describe the High Church side of Episcopal Church worship, as it had many of the same elements as the Roman Catholic Church. Such designations are rarely used anymore.

young man, he purchased a grand home in the heart of the town and erected a small chapel next to it. He was an Episcopalian, but he had the soul of an old-line Roman Catholic. He insisted that people attend private confession each week. Legend has it that on Sunday mornings, he would have his altar guild members standing at the door, making sure that each worshiper had indeed made his or her confession the prior week. If not, the person could not come in. When the lake was built in the 1920s and people started moving out to Sparta as summer residents, all the rules continued in place. If one was not used to private confession, he did not care. That person could not come to church! As time moved along, he gathered enough of a congregation that they were able to build a larger church a block or so away. He named it St. Mary's. He remained the Vicar for thirty-three years. It was the only church he ever served.

In 1954, he was succeeded by the Rev. Harold Shaffer. Like Fr. Ford, he was right out of seminary and continued the Anglo-Catholic tradition. He stayed for twenty-five years. In that time, a modern A-frame church was built in the residential neighborhood called - would you believe - Church Hill. Within a short period of time, the rectory and parish hall were added. After fifty-nine years as a mission, St. Mary's became a self-supporting parish, and Fr. Shaffer was named its first rector. This also was the only church he ever served and he retired in 1979.

There is a notion among clergy that after long ministries, it is not unusual for a new rector to have a somewhat short tenure. Making changes can be so difficult that once the changes occur, a general malaise overcomes the new rector and he needs to be on his way. I do not think that was the case for me. Even though I was there for only five years, if anything, I think the opposite was true. Yes, the church became a considerably different place in that time, but I think the new energy that was created made some people take a look at what was happening and encouraged me to consider other options for my life. I will explain all of that later.

It was evident that the congregation was ready for some serious changes. This was no longer the church of the old-line Anglo-Catholicism of Fr. Ford or even the more moderate Harold Shaffer. On top of that, Bishop Spong was inspiring a vision that people were responding to positively. We had just gained final approval of the 1979 Prayer Book, and the ordination of women and other great changes were in the air. It was an electric time in the Episcopal Church and nowhere more so than the Diocese of Newark.

I suspect the first hint that I was going to be a horse of a different color was that I did not own a black suit and usually only wore black clergy shirts on Sundays or on visits to the hospital. The pragmatic reality about clergy shirts is that I find them a little uncomfortable to wear. The stiff white plastic collars often pinch my neck. On another level, I found it distressing to have other men, and no small number of women, treat me deferentially. It was not unusual to have a woman hold the door for me to go through first. While I always dressed to professional standards, it was usually with a sports jacket, dress shirt and tie. I loved my profession and my calling, but I generally preferred for people to get to know me a little bit first before they began putting me into their own self-defined pigeonhole.

Secondly, I tried to gently discourage people from calling me Father. Of course, it is grammatically correct and appropriate for any priest, but I was afraid it would convey a context of authoritarianism. There was an old TV show called *Father Knows Best*, which was about a family headed by a loving, wise father. But I thought that in a church, this father did not always know best. I preferred to be seen as a partner of my congregation. I might have been presumptive enough to think that I knew better, but I did not know best. When adults called me Jim, I smiled and thanked them. When parents asked how their children should address me, I acknowledged that I thought "Mr. Sell" was a term of ample respect.[34]

In the five years that I was at St. Mary's, the Sunday attendance and annual giving doubled. When I arrived, the attendance was about 125 people. When I left, it averaged 250 people. I held on to several operating expectations for the life and ministry of the church. The first was that there needed to be some special event nearly every Sunday. It could be anything from an interesting adult forum to a new worship experience, a children's offering or a parish picnic. In other words, there had to be something happening all the time. Business as usual was not an option. This strategy required constant communication so that the congregation would know what was up.

Of course, that was before the days of e-mail, so we sent out weekly newsletters. It was an arduous task, but successful churches had to do it and do it well. You were required to write the material; type it onto a mimeograph stencil; run it on a mimeograph machine; collate, address, staple and stamp

---

[34] Episcopal clergy go quietly nuts when they are called by the adjective *reverend*. "Reverend Sell" is as grammatically incorrect as calling a judge "Honorable Jones," although it has devolved into common usage. The names the Rev. Mr. Sell, the Rev. James Sell, and the Rev. Fr. Sell all will pass the test of a junior high school grammar teacher.

each of the letters; and get them into the mail in a timely fashion. When I first arrived, my secretary seemed constantly flummoxed by all the tasks that fell to her. After a while, she moved on, and wonderful Judy Royce came more fully into my world. Judy grew up in Charleston a year behind me as Judy Higbee and attended Charleston Catholic High School. From there, she went to West Virginia University. She majored in home economics, but she was also a part-time secretary in the history department, where I spent much of my time. I do not recall meeting her in either high school or college, but our paths must have crossed over and over again. She married a pilot, moved to Sparta, became an Episcopalian, and was now in my congregation.

There is an ongoing discussion among my colleagues about whether it is appropriate to hire members of the church onto the staff. The reasons for not doing it almost always trump the reasons for doing it. It is easy to hire from within the congregation. Among other things, the learning curve for the new employee is far briefer than for someone unfamiliar with the uniquenesses of the church. But, it is nearly impossible to let a parishioner go! Judy was somebody I was comfortable with and she was good. To me, it was a perfect decision. Judy understood the importance of making sure the congregation was fully informed of the life and ministry of the church. Her father had been an editor for the *Charleston Daily Mail* newspaper. She came by her communication skills almost genetically.

We worked hard to find appropriate ways to celebrate our lives as Christians, as Episcopalians, and as a large community of friends. I wanted people to say to themselves that they better get to church each Sunday morning because something

important was happening and they were needed there. It
worked. All the while, the word was slowly leaking out that St.
Mary's Church was a great place for families and individuals.
If they came there, they would be made to feel welcome in no
time at all.

There was another center of gravity that I felt was important.
In the Episcopal Church, worship must be intelligent and
numinous. *Numinous* - now, there is a word for you. In short,
many people who go to church want to feel as if they have been
to church. Church is not a pop concert, a scholarly disputation,
or a Rotary meeting. It is something else. It is an opportunity
to get in touch with one's soul; to listen to the still, small voice
of God; and to be "in love and charity with one's neighbors
and intend to lead a new life, following in the commandments
of God by walking henceforth in God's holy way."[35] This is
not to say that Sunday morning must be stuffy or stiff. It had
better not be and it should not be boring or insulting either. The
use of a variety of musical and cultural metaphors can create
vitality and energy. The clergyperson can encourage a lot of
creativity in worship, provided he or she does not lose sight of
the objective. The days of going to church for social reasons are
long gone. People come to church because they want to come
to church! They do not need to be entertained. They want to be
enriched, inspired, spiritually-healed and renewed.

But there has to be a balance to being in a holy place that
seems beyond time and space. People want to feel as if they are
being spoken to personally and intimately. The era of the long-
winded, overweening sermon has thankfully slipped away, but
respect for the elegantly crafted sermon is still with us. The

---

[35] A phrase from the Book of Common Prayer.

quality of the preaching is critical. Nothing can destroy the best efforts of a church like a few bad sermons. Most people hardly notice if a soprano hits an occasional off-key note. That will probably not keep them away. But honest-to-God preaching will keep the people coming back and inviting their friends despite other complications.

As I said earlier, my role model was Frederick Buechner. He made complex subjects understandable by telling stories from his past that illustrated his points. After I got beyond my need to appear erudite, I learned to do the same thing. I virtually memorized what I wanted to say in advance so that my eye contact and engagement with the congregation were as personal as I could make them. Either I told stories about my experiences and myself, or I carefully crafted approximations of recollections from other stories I had heard. Sometimes I would simply describe one of the Biblical stories or one of Jesus's parables in a way that made a contemporary point. If there was a substantial national or international event, people expected me to place it in a meaningful religious or moral context. When I drifted off into theoretical concepts, the congregation would immediately start to lose interest. One of the most off-putting lines a preacher can throw out to his or her listeners is this: "When I was in seminary, I learned ..." People do not want textbook theology. They do not want rehashed academic lecture notes. They want something that comes straight from the heart. As soon as I got into a story, they were with me. Every story that is fundamentally true is an iconic story. It opens a window to the nature of faith and life. That is the magic of fairy stories, myths, legends, and folk tales. Of course, it is the power in Jesus's parables. They all carry universal themes that we know to be intrinsically true. I think that is the underlying secret to great preaching as well.

LIVING IN THE JOY OF FELLOWSHIP

We had a good time in St. Mary's Church. Several projects stand out. We had an annual summer auction the week-end before the Fourth of July. It was very big and very popular. It began decades ago when summer people would buy a cottage on the lake and needed to furnish it. Because St. Mary's finances were so tight, the vestry had an agreement with the fuel oil company that we would pay off whatever we owed on the prior winter's bill from the auction proceeds. Every year, we agonized over the weather. It was all outdoors and a rained out auction would have drowned us financially. It was a confirmed fact that it had not rained in Sparta on the Saturday before Independence Day for all of the dozens of years of that auction.[36] I did take advantage of any clout I might have with God and prayed mightily for no rain. Finally, in 1984, the church had grown so substantially that we were able to pay our fuel oil bill out of standard pledge and plate income. For the first time ever, we did not have to conduct the arduous auction if we did not want to. Immediately, we declared a moratorium. For at least one year, we would enjoy the week-end before Independence Day and take it easy. And, what happened? Throughout the entire week-end, it poured rain without let-up. God was saying, "Enough is enough!" I am not sure they ever had another auction again.

---

[36] Actually, around that time, the syndicated newspaper feature "Ripley's Believe It or Not" reported that "the annual fireman's parade in Ogdensburg, N.J." - three miles away and on exactly the same day as our auction - "had never been rained out in its entire 56 year history."

We found ourselves thrust into several international outreach programs. On one occasion, we hosted the immigration of a woman and her two sons who were supporters of the Shah of Iran when his government fell to the Islamic extremists. They had managed to walk out through the mountains and across the border of their country. We helped them get a new start in America.

On another occasion, we found ourselves being pulled into the orbit of the Rev. Jayapaul Daniel of the Church of South India. The story is long and complex, but a Sparta man was in a hospital in India. That hospital did not serve food. The families of the patients were expected to feed them. Of course, his family was far away, and there was no one to care for him. One day, as Jayapaul was passing through the hospital he saw the American, took pity on him, and made sure that he was fed. This man then learned that Jayapaul and his wife ran a home for children whose parents would not claim them. He returned to Sparta and told his story to Dick and Hattie Stone, who implored us to become involved with Jayapaul and his work. We did so. We even sprung for a trip to the United States for Jayapaul to have open-heart surgery in New Jersey. He stayed with parishioners while he recuperated. Sadly, a year later, he was traveling with others in a truck on a muddy road back in India when it turned over and he was killed.

In 1983, we learned that that the Diocese had a storage bin over in nearby Blairstown, filled with old, unclaimed church furniture. We asked the Diocesan officials if we might have the contents for our auction if we split our proceeds with them. I think they were pleased to get rid of the shed and save on the rental. We ended up with old pews, pulpits and all kinds of odd stuff. Amazingly, the items sold well. Among this trove was a tacky, fully painted four-foot-tall wooden statue of John the Baptist. There was no question who it was. The man was half-naked, wearing animal skins at his waist, and holding a shell, a symbol of baptism. He was in such poor taste; we decided he was too wonderful to get rid of. Instead, we concocted a plan: someone would take John home, and within a few days, that family would have to slip him onto the lawn of fellow parishioners. If John appeared on your lawn, you had to contribute at least one bag of groceries to our parish food bank. The activity was a huge success. People loved the game of waking up to find him on their lawn and then surreptitiously replanting him on another lawn. On one occasion, Ellen, the children, and I went out of town. Before we left, we drew the living room curtains closed over the large picture window of the rectory. When we returned in the early evening a few days later, we opened the curtains, and - zounds! - there was a half-dressed man standing there, looking in. It was just John the Baptist, paying us a visit in the gathering shadows!

I do not know what happened to him. He just disappeared. Either some family thought he was too beautiful for our parish games and stuck him in their basement, or perhaps someone thought we were not being duly respectful of this rare piece of religious art and turned him over to a more earnest church!

After I had been there about a year, the parishioners created something called the "Eating Out Club". We decided that sounded a little inappropriate (churches do not have clubs!), so the name was changed to "Chez Nous", or "At Our Home." Each year, names would be taken out of a list of interested people and assigned to dinner groups. It was then the job of these groups of eight or ten people to find times to get together to have dinner and build relationships. The groups were effective and a lot of fun. It was a great way to incorporate new worshipers. In 1985, Ellen and I were assigned to a group consisting of Nadine and Michael Sutcliffe, Bill and Denise Pearson, Hattie and Dick Stone, and Linda and Dave Sielken. Nearly thirty years later, we are still getting together. Sometimes we are joined by other St. Mary's alumni and, together, relive wonderful memories and pick up where we left off the last time we were together.

DEATH BY AIDS

We had two men in the congregation, Larry Brumfield and David Williams, who lived in a committed gay relationship. David was an ordained Methodist pastor who had been invited to step down from parish life because of his orientation. Larry had been a monk in a Catholic monastery in California. In other words, their Christian commitments were deep. They were admired and respected in every possible way by the congregation; they offered spiritual and intellectual leadership resources that we all appreciated. But they had a past. Before they became a couple, both of them had occasionally stepped into the distressed gay culture that led to one-night stands and impersonal sex. Somehow, someway, the slow and deadly HIV virus had gotten into their systems. At the time, I knew almost nothing about what that meant. The media was reporting conflicting interpretations about this deadly illness called AIDS. For years, Larry and David had avoided gay bars and other hangouts and both were living healthy, monogamous lives. One of the joys of my ministry was that in 1983, I was the first person I ever knew to bless a gay relationship. About a dozen people from the congregation met at their home and I honored their love in a carefully crafted Christian service.

One bitterly cold and snowy winter day, Ellen was stuck in a three-hour-long traffic jam on the mountain heading into Sparta caused by the storm. As she crept along, she looked over into the car across from her and saw David also stymied by the traffic. When she came to the exit ramp for Sparta, she observed that he continued on down the highway. We learned later that he was going to the hospital in Newton. He arrived there with about a 107-degree temperature and was dead in the morning. The immediate cause of his death was toxic shock with AIDS as the contributing cause. I say this respectfully: he could have struggled through one of the slow, horrible illnesses AIDS produces; at least he was spared that. His inevitable death was quick and relatively painless. Larry was inconsolable. David was cremated and buried in the parish columbarium. A large crowd of parishioners came.

The next day, the local newspaper ran a front page story that began, "Last night, AIDS took the life of the first citizen of Sussex County." It went on to identify David. I was shocked and angry at this violation of his privacy. I also had to deal with the fallout. Many of the congregation who had received Communion from the common chalice after him wondered whether that would enhance the likelihood that either they or their children would be infected. This was all so new. Most information about how the virus was transmitted seemed to indicate that the jury was still out. I immediately went to a highly esteemed physician and said to him, "You must give me the straight scoop. Are the members of my congregation in jeopardy or not? Do not sugarcoat this. I must have the clearest facts." He promised me that one could not get AIDS through a shared cup and said there was nothing for our congregation to be afraid of.

The next Sunday and for the next month or more, I repeated this information in every possible way to every possible worshiper. Thank God, there was no panic and life carried on as usual. We lost no members over that frightening moment.

Six months or so later, Larry disappeared. I could not find out where he went. There was no way for me to contact him. After some time, I heard that he had re-entered the gay community of New York City and surrounded himself with brothers who would care for him. And there he died as well. I wish we could have ministered to him as he was dying. I would have liked to comingle their cremated remains in our columbarium. It would have been a gracious tribute to honor these two fine men.

BEING CONNECTED

My years as a clergyperson in West Virginia had essentially been spent in a solo performance. I was far from professional colleagues; I usually had to try to figure things out for myself. My bishop, Bob Atkinson, was competent, wise, and kind. But he was one hundred miles west on a twisting mountain road and I only saw him when I was required to attend some kind of meeting.

After I had been in Sparta for a year or two, Leslie Smith proposed that a few of us who had come into the diocese at about the same time meet together in a mutually supportive colleague group. These were not my only clergy friends in northern New Jersey, but they became the ones to which I felt

most deeply bonded. Once a month for ten years, we met on
a rotating basis at one of our churches. There was no agenda.
Often the meeting was just backslapping and giving each other
attaboys. Certain stupid jokes seemed to reappear over and
over again. It was all part of being interconnected and mutually
respecting. Sometimes it was the only safe place we had to
vent our frustrations, shed a tear or ask for help. Three of them
became bishops, but on the other hand, several dropped out
of the ministry entirely. The lives of these fourteen men and
one woman have been fraught with pain and joy, success and
failure, but they have been full and filled with value.

As the church grew, I was able to have some fine clergy
assistance. The last year I was there, John Smiley became rector
of the church in Blairstown. When he arrived, he was joined
by his wife, Betsy, who was also ordained. After some budget
discussion by our vestry, we were able to call her to be our
assistant.

Betsy Dawn Inskeep Smiley was a wonder to behold. A
4.0 high school student, she had figured that if she wanted to
go to Harvard, she needed a sport. She took up marksmanship
and, despite her pacifist leanings, was a dead shot. Immediately
after college, she attended the Episcopal Divinity School in
Cambridge, Massachusetts, where she both met John and
prepared for ordination. I was not sure how the people of St.
Mary's would react to a female priest. After all, they were not
that far removed from the days of their male dominated Anglo-
Catholic history. My worry was unjustified. Her arrival was like
a bolt of lightning, but there was no thunder. They loved her.
She was gracious and faith-filled. She stayed on for a while after
I left. Some years later, John and Betsy moved to the Buffalo

area, where John was the Rector of the church in Orchard Park. There, Betsy developed a brain tumor and eventually died. Just thinking about her causes me to mourn again. I think she was the one clergyperson ever who could relate effectively to Andrew. Some years later, John remarried, and he is now the Bishop of Wyoming.

CHAPTER 6

ARCHDEACON

As the rector of St. Mary's, I was close to and supportive of Jack Spong. He was more than just my superior. He was a good friend whom I respectfully honored as the bishop. But soon after I arrived in Sparta, he began making my life a little complicated. I had been there just two years when he asked me if I would consider coming to work for him. Every diocese seems to have its own nomenclature for its staff employees. In the Diocese of Newark, the ordained administrative assistants are called Archdeacons. The titles of lay officers are usually determined by their positions; so for example, the person in charge of finances was called, duh, the Chief Financial Officer.

Usually, Jack had two Archdeacons. Together, they divided up deployment, parish development, communication, and program administration, as well as anything else that needed to be done. They were often among the first on the scene if there was a problem, such as a clergyperson who was acting out inappropriately or the hospitalization of a rector. There were

no Suffragan Bishops in the Diocese of Newark,[37] although
he did like to hire short term Assisting Bishops from time to
time. When he could invite one from an African or Hispanic
culture, it encouraged the heterogeneous ministry that existed
in northern New Jersey. Jack was a national figure in the church.
His books, lectures, and prophetic discourse were receiving a
wide audience. It was important for his staff to relieve him of
much of the day-to-day diocesan responsibilities as possible
so that he could fully engage in this important work. I think
what Jack saw in me was my experience as a newspaper writer
and my success in developing parish programs, not to mention
a friend who cared deeply about what he was doing. I hated
to refuse the offer, but I said to him that there was no way I
could leave St. Mary's after a mere two years. He agreed and
acknowledged that it was not a good idea.

After going through the usual interview process, he ended
up hiring an old friend and seminary dorm-mate of mine, Steve
Galleher, for the position. Steve was an inspired choice. He
was a rabid supporter of the philosophies and ministries of
Jack Spong and he was a crackerjack editor of the diocesan
newspaper *The Voice.*

---

[37] There are a variety of bishops in the Episcopal Church. The head of a
diocese is usually just called the Bishop. If a person is elected an assistant
bishop with the right to succession, he or she is called a Bishop Coadjutor,
as that bishop co-adjudicates with the head bishop. If someone is elected
an assistant bishop without the right to succession, he or she is called a
Suffragan Bishop. The word suffragan comes from a Latin word meaning
"supporting." Finally, sometimes a bishop retires or steps down from a
prior position and then gets hired by a new diocese as an aid to the head
bishop. That person is called an Assisting Bishop.

One day, Steve and I were talking and he made the point that the famous television weatherman on *The Today Show*, Willard Scott, and his wife, Mary, were personal friends of his. In my usual modest way (not), I said, "Well, if Ellen and I are your friends and Willard and Mary are your friends, why don't you and your wife, Lee, have us all for dinner with Jack and his wife, Joan?" And he did! On the appointed night, Jack and Joan Spong, Ellen and I, Willard and Mary, and Steve and Lee all gathered in a cozy little Brazilian restaurant in Manhattan. Of course, we needed to have dinner at around five o'clock, because Willard went to bed at about eight so that he could get up at four in the morning for *The Today Show*. We had the time of our lives. There were probably only another half dozen people in the restaurant at that time in the evening. They all sat there and watched everything we did as Willard regaled us with his boisterous charm and good humor. If you had watched Willard on television, you would have likely assumed he was a Baptist. He often dropped hints to that effect. In fact, he and Mary were committed Episcopalians.

Steve was going through a personal time of transition that was not easy for him. He could not fulfill the intense demands of his job. After about two years, he had to step aside, so Jack was back on the hunt for a new Archdeacon. By that time, I had been at St. Mary's for four years. Once again, he called and asked if I would consider interviewing for the position and once again, I said I did not feel it would be fair to the people of Sparta for me to leave so soon. I am not sure what happened in that ensuing year. I guess he muddled along as best he could with the staff he had while he looked for Steve's replacement. Finally, in early 1985, something happened that is part of the lore of our family. Some people had concocted a plan to raise money for some special diocesan ministry. They announced that they were going to hold the first annual Bishop's Ball. This gala event would be a "highlight of the diocesan social season and fun for all." It was not a good idea! There are a lot of other ways to have a good time in northern New Jersey besides going to an Episcopal Church dance. The first annual would also be the last annual. Despite a rather poor response, the event went on as planned. Ellen and I, the good scouts that we were, showed up even though I could not sell a single ticket to anyone else in my congregation. Halfway through the evening, Jack asked Ellen to dance. She returned to her seat with a thunderstruck look on her face. She said, "While we were dancing, Jack told me that he was down to two candidates for the vacant Archdeacon position but would throw them both out if you would agree to take the job." As I recall, after I found a moment to talk to him and make sure he was serious, I said that I needed a couple of days but would get back to him.

Ellen and I knew that this would be a considerable shift in our lives. I needed her support because accepting the offer would mean that I would be away from home far more than I had ever been. Part of the job of an Archdeacon is to be connected to parish clergy and provide support for them in their home congregations. It meant a lot of evenings and Sunday mornings away from Sparta and many late nights getting home.

By that time, Andrew was about fourteen and Katie was nine. Although it is generally seen as a bad idea for a former rector to remain in the town where he last served, this was going to be a requirement for me to take the job. I could not ask Ellen to move to another town and Andrew and Katie needed to have the continuity of the schools they were attending and the friendships they had created. However, we would have to buy a home and relocate because we were living in the church owned rectory of St. Mary's Church.

I was so keyed up about my interview that as I was getting in the car that morning to drive to the diocesan office in Newark, I left my briefcase on the roof of the car and took off down the street. Fortunately, I had not gone too far, when cars coming in the other direction started honking and pointing to my roof. Before disaster struck, I pulled over to the side of the road and retrieved my interview materials.

Jack had already made up his mind that he wanted to hire me but he insisted that the senior staff had to concur. The senior staff consisted of three people. Denise Haines, the other Archdeacon, was primarily responsible for deployment and parish development; that is, she would help match prospective clergy with vacant parishes and troubleshoot churches that were having internal issues. Christine Barney was the Chief Administrative Officer for the diocese. She managed a fairly large staff that included everyone from the cleaning crew to the secretarial personnel. John Zinn was the Chief Financial Officer. He and his bookkeeping staff had the enormous job of overseeing all the financial affairs of the diocese and insurance concerns of all the parishes and their employees. This was one of the ten largest dioceses in America and a lot was riding on his attention to detail. It was a great staff and I had an instant rapport with all of them.

Many clergy like to have their own sets of rituals and Jack Spong was no different. A couple of days later he called and said he wanted to come out to Sparta to talk to Ellen and me. I was pretty sure he was going to offer me the job, but since he wanted to come out there to talk, I thought maybe something had gone wrong. Nothing had gone wrong. It was just his custom never to offer a person a job over the phone. He wanted to do it in person at the candidate's home, if possible. He came out and offered me the job, which I accepted, and the three of us celebrated with a champagne toast.

The good news about our finances was that we owed nothing. The bad news was that we had nothing. Because we had always lived in church housing, we did not have one cent of equity to put down toward a new home. Jack arranged for me to receive a second mortgage from the diocese, which was used for a down payment. The diocesan Chancellor, Ward Herbert, one of the most highly esteemed attorneys in the state of New Jersey, served as our closing attorney pro bono. After some looking around, we found a nice split-level house a couple of miles away in the same school district and made the move.

The Senior Warden at St. Mary's was a special friend of mine. His name was Bill McGregor. He lived right across the street from us and was the stepfather of Lloyd and Wendy, the children who were early friends of Andrew's. Bill and I had organized a somewhat open membership poker club made up of men from the church. We called ourselves the "finance committee." (We played, hoping to finance ourselves, thank you!) He and I also played a lot of golf together, and I owned a personal pool cue which was kept at his home pool table. I felt badly when I had to tell him that I was leaving the church to work for the diocese. But Bill had spent his life in the corporate world and completely understood what I was doing. He took it all in stride. His wife, Norma, was the real estate broker who helped us find our new home. It was tough saying good-bye to St. Mary's. I knew I was leaving them earlier than I should, but they were gracious about it. They had a nice going away party for me. Besides, in some ways, we were not going far away. I stopped attending St. Mary's, but Ellen and the children remained active. My successor, Bob Dendtler, could not have been more supportive. He was effective as St. Mary's new rector and I bent over backward to be a strong, but unobtrusive, ally. We got along well.

It was about forty miles from my home to the office. On a good day, I could get there in less than an hour. If there was a traffic holdup, all bets were off. Every one of the core staff lived in a different county of northern New Jersey and we all had fairly rugged commutes. A number of us subscribed to books-on-tape and read as we drove along. We traded them around among ourselves and all got the benefit. During that time, I read a variety of current best sellers and some of the classics I had missed earlier in my life. There were a few occasions when I was known to arrive home in the evening from my commute but remain seated in my car in our driveway while I listened to the end of a gripping chapter in my current book. Ellen would ask the children if their father had gotten home yet and they would yawn and say, "Oh yes. He is sitting out in the driveway!"

My official title was Archdeacon for Program and Communication. The communication aspect is easy to describe. Once a month, we published a diocesan newspaper called *The Voice*. It had a wide readership because page two of its eight pages was always reserved for Jack's "op-ed" piece. Other bishops and clergy all over America subscribed to find out what he was currently thinking. It seemed that most of the great issues of church and society had their genesis or an early airing in our diocese. As the editor, I had to figure out what other material needed to be published, recruit authors, edit their work, and lay out the publication. I had a lot of help. There was a strong editorial board that took an active role, and I had the world's best administrative assistant in Gail Deckenbach. Gail had been working with the paper for a long time and knew far more about how to manage it than I did. She was my friend, teacher and facilitator. When I began, desktop publishing was just over the horizon, so we had to take the articles down to the local print shop, where they typeset them and made them ready for inclusion in our laid-out paper. From there, we would write headlines, add photographs, and try to produce a readable product. I had one other resource available to me: Leslie Smith, who kept coming into my life, had been a professional editor before he went to seminary. He could do this stuff with one arm tied behind his back. He loved coming in and giving me a hand. I would do the heavy lifting, and he would put on the many finishing touches that made the paper so attractive. The following year, we slowly began the process of adapting to desktop publishing. Gail would enter the material into the computer, and Leslie and I would lay it out from there.

We did it all well. There is a national organization called the Episcopal Communicators, and every year, they hold a convention. At that convention, they hand out awards for excellence in Episcopal journalism. In the years that I was the Archdeacon for Communication, we always snagged the most awards. Of course, having Jack, the Episcopal Church's number one communicator, writing for us every month helped a lot.

The other side of my job description was the program of the diocese. There was a whole catalogue of official diocesan programs. These were usually ministries that were too broadly based to be located within one congregation. For example, we had a prison ministry, a Hispanic ministry, a peace ministry, Cursillo, which was a kind of renewal ministry, a Union of Black Episcopalians, a resource center, a youth program called WOODY (World Of Our Diocesan Youth), an annual adult conference and a summer camp. These were the biggest programs, but another dozen or so vied for my attention from time to time.

There were some that I took an active role in, but I did not have to run any of them. I had to make sure that they had solid leadership, a clear vision, an active agenda and were properly funded. I spent a lot of time with the annual adult conference held each spring at Drew University in Madison. We drew such headliners as M. Scott Peck and Frederick Buechner. Along the same lines, Jack hosted a terrific series of four lectures a year called "New Dimensions." He would present one set each year and national figures would present the others. I had to make sure the many details of hosting celebrities were attended to. I gave my heart and soul to the summer camp, Eagle's Nest. And just to keep out of trouble, from time to time, I would step in and serve as a consultant to churches looking to find a new rector.

There was a certain synergy between program and communication, because it was important for me to be sure that these various program groups' work was properly promoted. When they were about to launch some special project, *The Voice* stood ready to do their publicity.

When I think over those days, I can hardly believe how rich they were. To have the honor of meeting people like Desmond Tutu, Caesar Chavez, Matthew Fox, Mortimer Adler, Buckminster Fuller, Madeline L'Engle, and many other amazing people who came through those offices was like a dream. Furthermore, to be connected to that wondrous staff was a joy.

CLOSING OLD CHAPTERS

I performed that job from 1985 to 1990. It was not that long of a time, but in some ways, it seemed like the most intense years of both my personal and professional lives. The Prayer Book says, "In the midst of life, we are in death." Not long after I began that job, I got a phone call from my mother in Charleston. I think it was the last conversation I ever had with her. She said, "Jim, I am not well. I am going to the hospital right now. I do not know what is wrong. Pray for me!"

It is all kind of a blur. The next morning, I jumped in the car and began making the five hundred mile drive south to Charleston. It began snowing somewhere in the mountains of western Maryland. I pulled into a truck stop late at night and asked for a bed. I do not know what normally went on in that bedroom. It was painted deep crimson and the bed rested on a platform in the middle of the room and had dark red sheets. I did not ask. The sheets were clean and I was exhausted. The next morning, there was a foot of snow outside, but the roads were plowed as I headed on to Charleston.

When I got to the hospital, Mother was intubated, so she could not talk, but she was alert and looked at me with longing, frightened eyes. Her doctor explained that she had septicemia, which is a way of saying she had blood poisoning. I do not think I ever got a complete explanation of what caused her condition. My research indicates that there could have been a number of possible causes. Maybe I did not even ask. I think I was too distraught. I sat there by her bed and held her hand and tried to talk, but since the conversation had to be one-sided, I did not have much to say. I tried to guess what she wanted to hear from me, but words failed. I told her that I loved her, would take care of Dad, and would surely see her later, which was meant to be openly interpreted as in heaven. In a little while, she drifted off to sleep and I went to their house for the night.

Dad was in a kind of daze. I understood that he was about to go through the biggest life change he had experienced in more than fifty years. However, there was more to the daze than I realized. I learned later that he was beginning to suffer early signs of dementia. Rather than let it be a source of concern for me and my sister, Mother had chosen to say nothing about it when she was well. It was in the very early stages. My mother's distress in dying was complicated by the fact that she was counting upon herself to be his caregiver. My promise to her to care for Dad was inviolate.

I do not remember whether I went back to the hospital the next morning or not. I did stop by St. John's Church and a funeral home that I was familiar with to explain the circumstances and make arrangements for her eventual cremation and funeral. I was concerned about getting back to my family and my new job and there did not seem to be any clear prognosis. Her doctor was not pessimistic. He thought she would get well. She could have gone on for months or years more as far as I understood. So I made my way back to Sparta, with snow falling all the way.

Every day, I called home and the information I received from Dad was sketchy at best. Finally, after about a week or so, he called and said rather flatly, "She's gone."

This time, all four of us drove to Charleston. I remember going down a hill in Pennsylvania and realizing that it was covered with black ice - ice that looks like rainwater. We were sliding out of control and I calmly said to the children, "Make sure your seat belts are tight. I cannot steer the car." Fortunately, we managed to drift to a stop before we hit anything or were hit. It was scary!

The funeral was sad, but Mother would have been pleased. There was a good-sized crowd at the service. We greeted and thanked them for coming in a reception in the church parish hall. She loved people and knew many Charlestonians. She was cremated and we took her remains to the Sell family plot at St. Matthew's Church in South Hills and scattered them there. Not much was done after that. Cappy and I spent some time with Dad. He seemed to be okay and able to take care of himself, so we all went back to our homes.

Within a month or so, I received a phone call from Dorothy Callicoat. The Callicoats were my parents' longest and dearest friends. Dorothy and my mother had once led their daughters' Brownie troop after the end of World War II. They were soul sisters. They had always been there for each other. Dorothy said that my father was having a hard time. He was feeding himself by walking several blocks away to a Baskin-Robbins store and living off ice cream. Ellen and I made a quick decision; he would have to move in with us.

In one bold move, Ellen took an airplane to Charleston, put the house on the market and arranged to have Buzzy Allen, our Ronceverte mover friend, clear out the house and bring the contents to Sparta. She then packed Dad in his car and drove him up to our house.

Some months after he died, we learned from a doctor that he had probably suffered from arteriosclerotic vascular disease (ASVD). This is often called hardening of the arteries. His dementia had a pattern that differed from a standard Alzheimer's disease diagnosis. Alzheimer's tends to be a fairly constant slow curve downhill. My father's condition consisted of small but sudden downward steps. When he first moved in with us, we were able to leave him during the day while the children went to school, Ellen taught and I commuted to Newark. We would leave lunch in the refrigerator and he would heat it up.

Then, one day, there was a substantial decline in his cognition. I was in my office. It was cold and rainy and I got a phone call. My neighbor across the street had found my father at his door, announcing that he had probably been kidnapped, because he did not know where he was. He was drenching wet and cold. To tell the truth, I have no idea how my neighbor found out how to contact me, but I was eternally grateful. I jumped in the car and got there in about an hour. I thanked him profusely. This was just the first chapter in a long series of painful and complex events we had as a family. To describe them in detail would serve no purpose.

We did not have a full grasp of what was going on, but it was clear that we needed to have someone stay with him during the day while we were gone. Our split-level house was fine for the four of us, but to bring him into it, along with custodial care, was about impossible. So we began thinking that we should relocate. Andrew had a classmate who lived in our old neighborhood in Church Hill. One day, he came home and said, "Ron Maisch's family is selling their house." We went up that evening, looked around and made an offer, which they accepted. It was a nice house with a fair price. Only a few days later did I realize that the house was yellow instead of white!

We moved in and had plenty of room for all of us, including Grandfather Sell and his caregivers. We first had one caregiver, then a second overnight shift, and, finally, twenty-four hour care. We sold the house in Charleston and he had some US Savings Bonds. We split the assets with Cappy and used what we received toward the new house. His condition kept deteriorating. Finally, he could not figure out how to eat or to swallow water. We put him in the hospital where they could give him nourishment. The social worker came by and I said I could not bring him back home. It was an enormous stress for every one of us, including him. I had been waiting for a nice room in a modern nursing home. There was no space available in any of the local facilities. However, the social worker said that he would be fine in a clean, well-managed older nursing home. I agreed and we put him in one a few blocks from the hospital in Newton.

Two days later, on a Friday, I went to see him and he spoke the first sentence I had heard from him in months. He probably did not know who I was, but he said to me, "I like my new apartment." I was relieved. Ellen had something to do that weekend, so I said to the children that after church on Sunday, we would drive over there and I would show them his room and let him see them. They had been troopers through this ordeal. There are no words to describe how proud I was of them. When we went in, the nurse said he was sitting in the dayroom, watching TV with some other men. We walked in and saw him sitting there, squeezed between two other residents. I knew instantly that he was dead. It almost seemed like he had forgotten how to breathe. I ushered the children out and called for the nurse, who confirmed my observation. We had no last rites or sorrowful good-byes. The man we knew had died months before. Exactly nine months to the day after my mother died, my father joined her in heaven. His death was a lonely moment for that lonely man. As the Prayer Book says, "Earth to earth. Ashes to ashes. Dust to dust." Within a day or two, he was cremated and we prepared to have him join my mother in St. Matthew's cemetery.

He is the only person I knew who had three funerals. The biggest one was at St. Mary's, Sparta. Many members of the congregation came to honor him. He had always said he wanted "When the Saints Go Marching In" sung at his funeral. Our brilliant organist, who had a baritone voice that could rock the walls, David Scott, blew us away with a solo rendition sung with solemnly paced dignity and hope. At a later time, Ellen and I had one of the stained-glass windows there dedicated to him. It portrayed Jesus healing the blind man. A smaller memorial service took place in the diocesan office. My colleagues gathered around me in sympathy. I offered my own remembrances, which were hard but healing.

Cappy and I and our families had a difficult time negotiating a mutually satisfactory time for his service in Charleston. Finally, after several weeks, we pulled it together. Of course, the obituary had appeared in the *Charleston Gazette* right after his death, but the date of the funeral had not been announced. By the time we got together, those who had gotten the word were few. The Rector of St. John's, Mary Adelia MacLeod, gave a fine sermon, calling him a man of "quiet dignity."

CHOATE ROSEMARY HALL

With his death and the settling of his estate, I actually had some money in the bank for the first time in my life. The first thing I did was buy a new Mazda Miata. This little sports car had just come onto the market and I had spent my life dreaming of having a car like it. Maybe it was my midlife crisis car. Maybe it was my mourning car. My fantasy was that I would drive it for a while and then give it to Andrew and Katie so that they would be cool high school superstars. No junky 1952 Nash Rambler for them! Andrew was learning to drive at the time and when I suggested that he should try the standard shift, there was nothing about it he liked. The car was too small, too hard to drive and, as he said in a memorable quote, "Not fun, Dad." Katie never warmed up to it either. Oh well. I kept it for another ten years or so and loved it.

But something else was brewing. In the fall of his freshman year, Andrew asked his mother if those conversations that had been bandied about in the past regarding boarding school were serious. She asked him why and he said that he was not feeling challenged at school. That evening, we talked about it. I renewed an old conversation, which was that his best shot would be Choate Rosemary Hall. However, there were two short-range problems: first, he was applying late, and second, he had to do well on the Secondary School Aptitude Test (SSAT).

It turned out that a round of SSATs was coming up and he could still apply to take them. I knew he was smart, but I did not guess how smart. He scored well and was completely qualified for a school like Choate, so he applied. We learned that even though his class had been admitted, they held four or five openings for people like Andrew, who were late to apply but exhibited strong qualifications. Of course, we used Seymour St. John and Bill Richardson as references. They both wrote supportive letters.

On the assigned weekend, Andrew and I drove up to Wallingford, Connecticut, for his interview. As we drove there, I conducted a little mock interview, asking him questions that I thought might come up. He was prepared and self-confident. When we got there, I was given a tour of the campus while he was interviewed and then the process switched. He saw the campus while I talked to the interviewer. His interviewer was a lovely woman named Diane Generous. What a fitting name, as far as we were concerned! When I was with her, she said, "We would like to offer your son admission and we hope that he will come."

I smiled politely and assured her that that was our wish as well. Deep in my heart, I was saying, *Don't these people know that we are just a generation or so away from rural Appalachian people, and this is amazing Choate?* I sure was not going to tell them. If Andrew had convinced them that he was a shining star, I had no intention of tarnishing his image.

On our way home, I said, "Andrew, what did she ask you?"

He said, "She asked me what I liked to do and I said I liked to cook. Then she asked me what I like to cook, and I told her I liked to make omelets. She asked me how to make an omelet, and I told her."

"That was the interview?" I queried.

"Yep," he said. "I think she just wanted to know if I could think through an idea and give a cogent answer."

The following fall, we drove Andrew to Choate Rosemary Hall for his sophomore year. I never cried when my parents died, but the tears quietly drifted down my cheeks as I pulled out of the parking lot. I loved being a father to both of my children more than anything else I ever did. I was so proud that he was on his way to a life that would be substantially different from anything I had ever known. I would not cry again for a transition such as this until a number of years later, when we bade Katie farewell as we put her on the airplane to go to El Salvador for three years in the Peace Corps. A person can pay a big price for loving others deeply.

Meanwhile, the good news was that we had a world-class daughter back at home. We all went through a kind of depression when Andrew left. Katie had come to rely on him as a friend, mentor and all-around good big brother. But as we had had Andrew all by himself for the first five years of his life, now we could have Katie for special bonding and love that we all looked forward to.

MEANWHILE, BACK AT THE DIOCESE

I had an amazing job. As I think about it, the five years that I was in the office of the Diocese of Newark were as significant as any time and place in the history of the American Episcopal Church. Two of the principal players, the Rt. Rev. Jack Spong and the Rt. Rev. Walter Righter, have chronicled the events that were so compelling with greater detail than I ever could. Jack's autobiography, *Here I Stand: My Struggle for A Christianity of*

Integrity, Love, and Equality[38] and Walter Righter's *A Pilgrim's Way*[39] describe these years with great honesty and accuracy. What I would like to do is look at some of the most riveting events from my own little fly-on-the-wall perspective.

I cannot be sure that I will get the chronology exactly right but I can hold the story together. The first recollection I want to share is the coming of a new co-Archdeacon and colleague for me. Not long after I arrived, Denise Haines made a decision that she wished to return to the ministry that had been her passion: hospital chaplaincy. She announced that she would be leaving the diocesan staff. Jack came by to give me this news and asked me if I knew anyone who might be interested and available to take her position. Turnabout is fair play. I immediately suggested Leslie Smith. At that point, Leslie had been in Bloomfield/Glen Ridge for seven years. He had been my colleague, friend, classmate, and brother who is not my brother. Jack was happy to extend an invitation to him, which Leslie readily accepted. I was thrilled. Leslie had reached out to me in many gracious ways. To be able to reciprocate a little bit was wonderful.

As I already noted, Leslie was a skilled editor. We immediately became a team. I would plan the contents of *The Voice*, and he would orchestrate its layout. I continued on with the program arm of the diocese. Leslie was responsible for deployment. Both of us did whatever else had to be done. Along with everything else, I took a stint as Acting Dean of the Cathedral in Newark for a year. It was an honor for me to be so completely accepted by this totally black congregation.

---

[38] Harper Collins, San Francisco (1999)
[39] Knopf, New York (!998)

That was when I talked Jack into getting arrested with me on the streets of New York for protesting the South African policy of apartheid. The ride in the paddy wagon was a great memory, but our lawyer was waiting at the court house to spring us as soon as we were ushered in. With Christine Barney and John Zinn handling the nuts and bolts of the diocese and Leslie and I keeping the wheels running, Jack was able to engage the great issues of the church.

During that time, the Rt. Rev. Walter C. Righter, the retired Bishop of Iowa, accepted Jack's invitation to serve as an Assisting Bishop. This choice was atypical for Jack. He liked to have Third World bishops come to Newark for three to six months. He gave them an opportunity to have a kind of extended sabbatical, while we had the benefit of their cultural diversity. At first blush, Walter looked like a basic "good ole boy" from the Midwest. He was, but also he was not.

Something else was going on during that time. Again, all of this is carefully documented by Jack in his autobiography. His wife, Joan, was suffering from classic paranoia. It is a sad disease. In many ways, she could function well in day-to-day life, but she was haunted by fears of oppression by groups like the CIA and the FBI. Life got so complex for Jack that he was forced to move into a small apartment the diocese owned that was next door to our offices. On a regular basis, he would drive out to Morristown, where he and Joan had their home, to make sure she was provided for. It was not a happy existence. On one memorable occasion, he was accosted by a street person armed with a broken bottle who tried to rob him. After Jack fended him off, taking him to the ground (Jack is a big guy!)

and forcing him to surrender his weapon, Jack turned around and still gave the shocked perpetrator some money!

As Joan's condition deteriorated, the doctors discovered that she also had breast cancer. The whole situation was complicated and tragic. Despite his entreaties, she was resistant to continued aggressive therapy, as she was terrified of the prospects of being put to sleep against her will. Jack has three adult daughters and two of them agreed to invite Joan to Richmond, where they lived and where Jack had been before he was elected bishop. She was happy to go there, so Jack packed her up and took her to live near their daughters.

Within a fairly brief period of time, Joan died in Richmond. I only tell the following story because Jack tells it and because I watched the whole thing. A number of us went to St. Paul's Church, Richmond for the funeral. As we entered the church, I witnessed one of the most bizarre and repugnant displays of behavior I have ever encountered. Jack was walking ahead of me with his daughters, when an elderly woman who looked as if she could have been a mourner, leaped up out of her pew, slammed her umbrella across Jack's back, and said, "You son of a bitch. I have wanted to tell you what I have been thinking of you for a long time. I finally get the chance." I do not think we ever learned who the perpetrator was. She was hurried out of the church and we never saw her again. We were all thunderstruck. Here was a man grieving over the death of his wife and this old crone had the temerity to attack him at this most vulnerable moment.

Ordaining Gay Men

As anyone who had the slightest openness to the subject understands, the church has been ordaining gay men for as long as the Christian ministry has been around. The complication of going into much of a conversation about its history is that the past was shrouded in rumor, denial, and suspicion. In some instances, the bishops knew of their orientation and told them to keep it quiet. Others simply did not ask, preferring to live in a state of benign unknowing. Most church members claimed they were opposed to such a thing but willingly accepted it, if it was kept under wraps. In some cases, a marriage of convenience was arranged so that the man could be ordained without raising suspicion, providing a lifetime of pain and failure for both him and his wife. The history of gay ordination was sordid and without redeeming merit. Curiously, ordaining lesbian woman was a little easier. The first lesbian woman I recall being ordained a priest was Ellen Barrett. In 1977, Bishop Paul Moore ordained her in the Diocese of New York. I never knew Ellen, but she had been a counselor at a camp in Greenbrier County, West Virginia, a few years before I lived there.[40]

While I was an Archdeacon, Jack determined that the subject of gay ordination needed to come into the open. After plenty of consultation and evaluation, he invited Robert Williams to be the first openly gay man to be ordained. A Texan who was an iconoclast, Robert happily accepted the offer, but I had another candidate but could not seem to push him to the front of the line. I will say more about that in a minute. Robert was ordained

---

[40] See Paul Moore Jr., *Take a Bishop Like Me*, Harper and Row, New York (1979).

a priest in 1988. My loyalty to the Diocese of Newark was deep, but I could not bring myself to go to Robert's ordination. I found him so offensive on so many levels that I could not see how he could be the proper face of a new age in the Episcopal Church. Within days, my greatest fears were realized. With his ordination, Robert had a national platform, but his comments in the media were so rude that Jack had no other recourse than to revoke his ordination. It was a horrible time in our lives. Here Jack was trying to do something constructive and progressive and he was betrayed in the most fundamental way.

Meanwhile, Dale Hart, a member of my staff, was serving as the Director of the Bishop Anand Resource Center. The resource center provides video, digital and printed resources for parishes and individuals throughout the diocese. One day, she came in and said that she was going to have to move on. After thanking her for her great service, I asked her if she had any suggestions for her replacement. She told me about a young man named Barry Stopfel. Barry was a member of her church in Ridgewood and was studying at Union Theological Seminary in New York City. He was not exactly on a track toward ordination, because he was living in a gay relationship with his partner, Will Leckie. Sometimes I think I am one degree of separation from everyone - I did not know Will, but I knew his father, who was a coal businessman in western Greenbrier County.

I called Barry and invited him to come see me. He did and I immediately offered him the job, contingent upon Jack's final approval. He proved to be a terrific employee. While he yearned for ordination, he was too modest to push the boundaries. When I proposed to Jack that Barry would be a wonderful first candidate for ordination as a gay priest, Jack's mind was already made up and I could not change it. As soon as Robert imploded, I re-entered the conversation with my dark horse candidate, Barry. Time had marched on, and Jack was preparing to go on a sabbatical. When it was suggested that maybe Walter Righter might ordain Barry, both Jack and Walter agreed.

Barry was never going to be the bold public face of gay ordination. Reserved, pastoral, and gentle, he was just yearning to be a parish priest. Not long after his ordination, he was called to the church in Maplewood. He served a distinguished ministry there. However, the turmoil was not over. Jack had left his office on his sabbatical and Walter had risen to the occasion and ordained Barry. Now, any reasonably smart bishop knew better than to get into a debate with Jack Spong. He is far too agile and articulate for any average adversary. There had been rumblings of recriminations from a few bishops when Jack ordained Robert Williams. That was it - just rumblings. Nothing came of them. But once good old easygoing Walter ordained modest, self-effacing Barry, antagonistic forces in the House of Bishops believed they could score some points in opposition. Much of the following finally was resolved after I had left my job. But Walter's book describes his heresy trial (yes, heresy trial!) accurately. The Chancellor or attorney of the diocese at the time was Mike Rehill. Mike did not seem to fit the standard image of a Diocese of Newark warrior, as he was an Anglo-Catholic and politically conservative. But he was also a scrupulous lawyer. He believed in defending his clients to the full extent of his ability. Walter was presented with a charge of heresy by the House of Bishops and ordered to stand trial as for ordaining Barry Stopfel. I am not making this up. It was about as ludicrous a thing to happen as anything in modern Christianity. What were they going to do? Lash him to a stake and set him on fire? Walter and Mike made them look like fools. Walter was found innocent, and perhaps of greater consequence, any conversation about ordaining gay persons was crushed forever.[41]

CAMPING

One of the lesser-known items on my résumé was that I had spent many summers as a camper, staff member, and camp promoter. As a child, I often went to several camps in the same summer. After I was ordained and living in West Virginia, I was on the clergy staff of Peterkin, an Episcopal Church camp, every summer for about nine years.[42] That is not to say I spent all summer at these camps. I would take a week or two to help out with the program. Once I arrived in the Diocese of Newark, I served as the chair of the camp board of directors. The name of the camp was Eagle's Nest. In 1980, that camp was located on a little strip of land along the Delaware River. It had had a long and effective history, but it was being physically impacted by a number of nearby commercial ventures. It became clear that it was no longer going to be a suitable venue.

---

[41] To get Barry and Will's perspective on all of this, see, *Courage to Love: A Gay Priest Stands Up for His Beliefs,* Barry Stopfel and Will Leckie, Doubleday, New York (1997)

[42] It was there that I had the experience of getting to know a delightful young camper from eastern West Virginia named Henry Louis Gates Jr. He was funny and smart. Skip Gates went on to become one of America's great scholars, chair of the African American studies program at Harvard, and a legend in his own time. Amazing.

Jack had conducted a large and successful capital campaign in the early '80s. A piece of that campaign was a goal of developing a new Eagle's Nest. The diocese was given a large tract of land for the camp. Unfortunately, our consultants uniformly agreed that it was never going to be a developable piece of property. After looking at a number of other properties, I proposed that we rent an existing camp in central Sussex County. I had no concern about where it was located, but since it was about fifteen miles from my home, it turned out to be a great location for me personally. Once I became the Archdeacon, I was able to go up to the camp once or twice a week during the summers instead of driving to Newark.

The age of Episcopal Church camping seems to be ebbing away. I regret that. Many campers built lifelong attachments to one another and to the church through that experience. My undergirding philosophy was that the diocese should operate a program that provided all the fun of a summer camp along with a soft emphasis on Christian education. We were not interested in making our children into little religious zealots, but we did want them to have a positive attitude about the church and its teachings.

My first director was Kathryn King. The daughter of an Episcopal clergy family and someone deeply immersed in the ministry of northern New Jersey Episcopalians, she was a natural and, if I may so, an excellent choice. The blessing of living in northern New Jersey is that the cultural diversity is staggering. The challenge of living in northern New Jersey is that the cultural diversity is staggering. We had upper-middle-class congregations in exclusive suburbs, distressed churches in the heart of some of America's most troubled cities, and just about everything else in between. My goal was to serve them all. We wanted both our privileged and our poor children to have a shared life together in a wonderful outdoor setting. I believed that the cross-fertilization of these communities would be a valuable learning experience all by itself.

The first challenge Kathryn had was to assemble a multicultural, multiethnic, and multitalented staff of counselors. She hit a home run. She had bright college kids from well-to-do communities and young adults from difficult circumstances. They got along beautifully, accepted one another fully and set a tone of mutual caring and sharing that translated into a highly effective camp for the kids.

Of course, many of our kids did not have the money to pay for camp. We expected every family to pay something, but we were not in the business of trying to make a profit. When we could get churches to help with our budget, we were appreciative. Diocesan resources were a big help. I do not know how we did it sometimes, but we always got by, paid our counselors, and made it all work.

As far as my own family was concerned, this was not Andrew's cup of tea. His heart was not in the camping life. One day, when Katie was eight (a year before she was eligible to attend), I took her up for a day and she would not leave. She loved it! She attended every summer until we moved away. That cultural experience was a defining period of her young life. When she went on to college, majored in anthropology and volunteered for the Peace Corps to go to El Salvador and live high up in the mountains with the poor, I felt as if her Eagle's Nest days had born rich fruit.

The camp continued after I stepped down as Archdeacon. It merged with the camping program in the Diocese of New Jersey and, later, the Lutherans. It was relocated to another place as well. Katie continues to stay connected to some of its alumni, but I have lost touch with them.

RUNNING FOR BISHOP

Like all clergy, good bishops are a gracious asset and incompetent ones are a drain on the church. I have been blessed with more good ones than bad ones. When I think of the ones I liked working under, of course, Jack Spong leads the list. He did many things well. His vision for the church was bold but achievable. As I have said, he was a great recruiter of clergy. He was a successful fundraiser. He challenged clergy to excellence and the good ones responded. He would actively support the ministries of clergy he was theologically different from because he sincerely valued diversity. He worked hard, paid attention to details and made sure the needs of parishes were being met. While I was there, just about every church in his diocese paid its full asking assessment[43] year in and year out. That was no small affirmation of his leadership!

There were a lot of other good bishops, too. Of those I served under, most were all at the top of my personal hit parade. There were many others with whom I had a tangential relationship.

---

[43] Every diocese has some kind of system for receiving financial support from its parishes. This income funds everything from national church programs to summer camps and resource centers. In my early years, parishes were assigned an amount based on a percentage of their annual budgets. Later on, a voluntary system became more commonplace—and less successful.

They did admirable jobs, but my life with them was somewhat limited. On occasion, something can go wrong. Like an ill-fitting priest in a congregation, a bishop who gets elected just because he or she is a convenient choice among the nominated candidates can do harm that can last for decades into the future. I suffered with a couple of those as well.

As far as my own aspirations for the office were concerned, you have to understand that I loved the parish ministry. I loved preaching to the same people week in and week out. I considered it a privilege to be invited into the lives of people at moments of sadness and joy. I never tired of the ebb and flow of the church year, with the high seasons of Easter and Christmas and the contemplative periods of Lent and Advent. I wrapped myself with a large circle of friends that other clergy call parishioners and together we explored the mysteries of God's almighty hand. Bishops are generally outside those spiritual intimacies because they are not connected to a congregation. However, there was a period in my life when the spotlight of the episcopacy began to shine upon me. Much of this was Jack's doing. He wanted his clergy to do well and he made every effort to enable their successes. He made the decision that if I was going to leave the Diocese of Newark, I should do so as a bishop.

There is a kind of art and science of being elected a bishop. A prospective candidate might be nominated in one diocese and not get elected there unless he or she has some deeply rooted history within it. Being a candidate in one diocese often encourages other dioceses to take a look to consider whether that priest might have the skills required in their own election. Perhaps the second or third time as a candidate, lightning might strike.

The election process is cumbersome and difficult. First, there is a nominating committee that selects qualified candidates. Then there is a period of information sharing, when the candidates are bused around the diocese to meet the designated voters. In the Episcopal Church, a clergyperson must be elected by a majority of both the lay votes and the clergy votes. When the election convention is held, balloting begins and it continues until one candidate receives a majority of votes in both houses of voters. A typical election might go on for four or five ballots. One ballot is not unheard of. Twenty or more have been known to take place.

The first time I was considered was in the Diocese of Southern Ohio. This represents approximately the southern half of the state of Ohio. Its central offices are located in Cincinnati. Part way through their preliminary process, they pared down their candidates from seven prospects to five. I was one of the two who did not make the final cut. However, even then, my name rose in national visibility.

Some months later, I was considered and nominated in the Diocese of Central Florida. Orlando is the seat of that diocese. I do not know why I was put on their ballot. There was nothing on my résumé that would have suggested that I would be a good bishop for those people. I think I was nominated to show the world that their diocese was not monochromatically conservative. I knew I did not have a chance. However, just before that election, I was also nominated in the Diocese of Southern Virginia. *Now,* I thought, *there is a place I might fit in.* I consider myself a *via media* standard-brand Episcopalian, moderate in affairs of church life but fiscally cautious. That was not what I saw in Central Florida, but Southern Virginia seemed to have those markings.

I stayed in the election in Central Florida for one primary reason: I wanted to engage those people and find out what kinds of questions and concerns they had. It was clear that I was nominated because I was Jack Spong's Archdeacon and he was the most prominent bishop in America. It was also clear that I was not going to get elected there for the same reason. Jack Spong was too much of an unpredictable entity for them and I was seen to be like him. I could not have been more proud! I received one vote!

A month later, I was right back in the thick of it in Southern Virginia. The word on the street was that I was going to be a strong candidate. I could tell during the bus ride and my various evening conversations that people were interested in me. In Florida, when I would speak, they would just walk away. In Virginia, they hung around to ask follow-up questions and were clearly engaged. There were five candidates, but one of them, Frank Vest, had a lock on it. He was from Virginia, he was well known and he was already a bishop, serving as a Suffragan in North Carolina. When the election was held and I won a plurality of votes among the clergy and he won a plurality of votes among the laity, the race quickly came down to the two of us. After a couple of more ballots, Frank won the whole election and was their new bishop. I liked Frank immensely and he was a fine bishop. A few years later, he was considered as a candidate for Presiding Bishop, the top position in the American Episcopal Church.

Something profound happened to me in that election. I felt as if I were being called not to be a bishop but to move back into being a parish priest. Being a bishop is a great honor, but it is fraught with frustrations and complications. You get all the heartbreak and little of the personal satisfaction of being intimately engaged in the lives of other people. In the years that followed, sexual misconduct became rampant and bishops were forced to take extreme measures in dealing with this crisis. That was a stressful time. Also, as time moved on, a major demographic shift of people away from church life came along and the stresses placed on bishops became acute. I believe God loved Jim Sell too much to place those burdens upon him. I made a decision after the Southern Virginia election that I would never run for bishop again. It was the right choice for me.

WEDDING BELLS

When Joan Spong died, Jack was surrounded by people who loved him and cared about him. His staff was the first team. We all sought to be as sensitive and supportive as we could. but none of us had the skills of Christine Barney. Chris had known Jack and Joan through her membership at St. Peter's Church, Morristown. She had been a friend of Joan and was able to be a pastoral presence in the midst of those difficult days. She was also the principal administrator of the diocesan offices. She managed all the day-to-day matters outside of finances. Born and raised in England, she had married an American airline pilot and relocated to New Jersey. After she and her husband raised two children, her marriage ended.

In a relationship that I would define as both beautiful and appropriate, Jack and Christine's mutual support and friendship developed into a deep bonding. I loved being on the sidelines and quietly cheering them on as they grew more in love with one another. It was a great joy to all of their families and to the staff when Jack asked Christine to marry him. The wedding was held at St. Peter's. Leslie was the preacher and I was the celebrant at the Eucharist. If ever there was a marriage made in heaven, it was Jack and Christine Spong's. The good old Prayer Book has the right words for it once again: "Those who God has joined together let no one put asunder."

CHAPTER 7

LEAVING NEW JERSEY

Two converging realities came about because I was nominated for bishop in the Diocese of Southern Virginia. The first was that I came to understand that what I was best at doing was being the rector of a church. Despite its occasional frustrations and stresses, I was made for that work. Before I started my freshman year in college, I took a Kuder Preference Test to determine where I might excel in a career. At the time, I thought the outcome was humorous. My highest score was to be the executive director of a chamber of commerce. I now know that test was remarkably accurate. An executive director of a chamber of commerce has to be able to juggle the multiple interests and demands of a wide variety of self-involved member organizations. At the same time, he or she must be gracious and accepting of all of them while keeping his own agenda carefully reined in. He or she must always try to beat the drum for his organization and inspire and encourage its growth and success. That is just about the job description of the rector of a thriving parish. Every day that I entered the office of every parish ever I served, I never knew what was going to happen. From being with someone who was dying to attending to a leaking roof, the variety of experiences was unpredictable and diverse. It was important that I always tried to subjugate my needs to those of the parishioners. As I said in an earlier chapter, I seem to be driven toward growth and development. Those interests probably look better in a chamber of commerce director, but they are usable in a parish as well. Since I had sworn never to run for bishop again, I began thinking about a church I could move to for a long period of time where I could make a significant difference. While I thrived as an archdeacon, it was one degree of separation away from what I really wanted to do which was to be the rector of a parish church.

The second discovery from my sojourn among bishop elections was the Diocese of Southern Virginia. I found the geography of the greater Norfolk area to be appealing (lots of water and not much really cold weather!). The bishop of the diocese, Charles Vache, and his new coadjutor, Frank Vest, seemed to be the kind of leaders I could respect. An unintended consequence of my nomination in Southern Virginia was that Christ and St. Luke's Church in downtown Norfolk was looking for a rector and I was added to their list of candidates. Some of the people from that church had a chance to hear me speak and felt that I might be a match for their needs. Within a few months, I received an inquiry from them, asking if I might be willing to be interviewed. I first consulted with Ellen and Katie and they were supportive. By that time, Andrew was a senior in high school and on his way to Georgetown University. He was interested but not personally invested in this decision. I also talked to Charles Vache and explained to him that if I were to end up coming there, Frank Vest would never have to worry about my presence in the diocese. Having been Frank's chief competition for bishop, he might have had some concern about

whether I was going to meddle in his affairs. I do not think I
ever did. I certainly did not want to. I wanted to be his support
in all matters.

Christ and St. Luke's was not without its blemishes. Through
the 1960s and '70s, it had prospered, but in its most recent years,
it had suffered an enormous downsizing of membership. The
budget was about half of what the church needed for a minimal
program life. The church building itself, however, was a work
of art. The congregation dated back to 1636 and this was their
fourth building. Designed by the architectural firm of Watson
and Huckle of Philadelphia, in the tradition of Ralph Adams
Cram,[44] it was built at the end of the neo-Gothic revival era
in American church architecture. It is a magnificent structure
that sits overlooking a bay of water known as The Hague in a
neighborhood called Ghent. Its windows were executed by a
firm from Germany and patterned after those in the cathedral
at Cologne. Originally intended to be the cathedral of the
Diocese of Southern Virginia, the work was inaugurated in
1909 with the President of the United States, William Howard
Taft, in attendance at the laying of the cornerstone. Becoming
a cathedral never happened. Back then, southern Virginians
seemed to think that cathedrals were too prissy for their
Protestant-oriented life, so the idea was rejected. In the 1960s,
the church installed one of the greatest organs in America and
became known for its extraordinary musical program.

At one point, the church was just called Christ Church. But
when St. Luke's Church, a mere six or so blocks away, burned
down in the 1930s, the bishop at the time merged them. Despite

---

[44] The designer of the National Cathedral and the godfather of the so-called
neo-Gothic revival of late nineteenth century America.

the congregations' mutual disapproval, it turned out to be the right thing to do. St. Luke's received a considerable insurance payout from the fire. That money allowed Christ Church to pay off the debt it still had owing from its construction mortgages. Legend has it that for twenty years, St. Luke's people sat on one side of the church and Christ Church people sat on the other.

CHRIST AND ST. LUKE'S, NORFOLK, VIRGINIA

The chair of the search committee was a lovely man named David Dashiell. A retired banker, he had the time to attend to the many complications involved in finding a new rector. He assembled a fine team of people whom I greatly admired. Despite their best efforts, it was not easy for them to call me. A couple of vestry officers were upset that they would actually call someone who worked for Jack Spong. They went to the bishop and complained. They made it clear that while they did not know me, I was not acceptable. Even though I was called and accepted, they vowed do whatever it would take for me to have a brief tenure. A senior member of the vestry came by my office one day in the first month or so that I was there and said quite bluntly, "I do not want you here and I want you to leave as soon as possible." They insisted that I be paid no more than what I had been earning in New Jersey. I was the lowest paid senior clergyperson in the diocese and that never changed. I stayed for fifteen years. They did not understand that a three on the Enneagram would never walk away! And a kid with the challenges of dyslexia stayed put until he got done what he wanted to get done!

I do not know what the worst timing in my life was. Moving from Lewisburg to Sparta was distressing to Andrew. He had been a happy little boy, and suddenly, it seemed as if he had to rewind his life all over again. This time, Katie had to endure the worst of the move. She made great grades, had a lot of friends and loved her summers at Eagle's Nest. Suddenly, she was thrust into a new world where friendships were already made and she was the newcomer. That was not all. Once again, I had done what I had promised I would never do again. I forced Ellen out of her comfort zone and into a whole new place. One of the conditions of my accepting the call was that Ellen needed to find a teaching job. The search committee put on a full-court press and lined her up with three different Latin teaching interviews. The most attractive position was at the middle school of Norfolk Academy, an old and highly esteemed private day school. She was immediately recognized as a master teacher and ended up having a long and satisfying career there.

At the time, Norfolk Academy was willing to accept the children of a teacher, provided they could do the work. Of course, Katie could do the work, so in the fall of 1990, she enrolled as an eighth grader. Meanwhile, the day that we moved to Norfolk was Andrew's first day as a student at Georgetown University in Washington, DC, majoring in international relations.

Ellen and I had come down to Norfolk to look for a house to buy. I virtually abstained from making a decision. After dragging her away from her happy home in Sparta, I felt the least I could do was let her pick something that satisfied her. Nothing came along that worked, so we initially rented a home in an area known as Larchmont. It was small, but it worked for the time being. This was in a period of slow housing sales

across the country, so when our house sold right away in
Sparta, we were both surprised and relieved. We knew that we
would have to make a purchase to reinvest our equity. With the
combination of Ellen's frustration about moving and her natural
tendency toward caution, we managed to go through three real
estate agents and spent the better part of a year looking around.
We arrived in June and in December, we were invited to a
Christmas tree lighting in a neighborhood called West Ghent.
I did not even know West Ghent existed, even though it was
within a mile or two of the church. I think we both decided that
was the right neighborhood for us. My memory is that Ellen
looked at every house for sale in West Ghent until we settled
on one on Westover Avenue. It had been in the same family
for many decades and was tired, so we hired a contractor, who
spent months remodeling and restoring it. In the end, we had a
comfortable home in a charming urban neighborhood. Christ
and St. Luke's did not have a large endowment for its size and
history, but they had sold their rectory a few years before and
invested the receipts into something called the rector's housing
fund. That provided income to help several of my assistants and
me to purchase homes.

Christ and St. Luke's was not an easy place, despite my
reputation for being something of a turnaround specialist.
Frankly, there was not a lot to work with. When I first came,
there were three services: an eight o'clock Rite I, a tired and
dated nine-thirty Rite II folk mass that had been on summer
vacation, and an eleven o'clock Rite I service with choir. I
immediately disbanded the nine-thirty service and merged it
with the eleven o'clock service at ten fifteen. It became a Rite II
service with choir. At the end of that summer, we were having

about 25 people at eight o'clock and 125 people at ten o'clock, including the choir, a few of whom were paid to be there. This was in a church that held six hundred to eight hundred people. I came home from church one day and Ellen said to me, "Can you tell me why we came here?" Almost in tears, I did not have an answer.

Perhaps that same Sunday evening, Katie went to the first youth group meeting of the fall and there were three other teens. She had been used to several dozen in Sparta. She looked at me with forlorn eyes as if also to say, "Can you tell me why we came here, Dad?" I wanted the ground to open up and swallow me. On top of that, those officers of the vestry who felt as if they had been forced to take what they perceived to be an eastern moderate were resistive to everything I did.

Fortunately, I did have a few things going for me. The search committee was 100 percent loyal and committed to being my fellow travelers into the future. Secondly, although there was almost no staff for such an operation, I did have a wonderful part-time secretary and full-time friend in Betty Denniston, a loyal sexton (a church word for janitor) and security officer in David Roberts[45] and a part-time organist in Allen Schaffer. Allen was a full professor at Norfolk State University and had fine musical training and considerable experience. He had been

---

[45] Our building was broken into constantly. I would get calls from the police every few months. We knew the nature of the vulnerability of the building but were too broke to do anything about it. The same was true about handicap accessibility. It did not exist. Our telephone system was so antiquated that the most efficient way to transfer a call was to yell down the hall for the correct recipient to pick up. I always kept a roll of toilet tissue in my desk because we could not rely on its availability in the restrooms. The church could not afford to attend to these fundamental matters.

the assistant to Grover Oberle, the former organist, for nine years. When I arrived, he was the acting organist, awaiting my nomination of him to the tenured position of organist and choirmaster. These were the good people who weathered the next year or two with me as we began to bring some new life into the church's ministry. But our budget was so low that I was not sure if we could develop much of a program.

The first thing I insisted we do was restore the nursery and hire child care personnel to take care of the children during worship. When the resistive element said that was a waste of money because the church had no little children, I said the obvious: "I wonder why there are no children." I was sure I had made a bad mistake in coming there and making the two women in my life that I loved the most suffer such indignities.

Then something happened that made my hopes begin to turn around. One day, Win Lewis, a priest ten years younger than I who was serving a small church in Hampton but had been a Curate (assistant) at Christ's and St. Luke's some years earlier, called and asked if we could have lunch. I was happy to have lunch with Win. I felt he would have some good oral history to share with me. We had a great time together. He said he had been a supporter of mine in the recent election and was sorry I had not won. Then, a couple of weeks later, into the office popped his fabulous wife, Cathy. She had just begun working as a talk show host for WHRO, the local public radio station. I do not remember much about that visit, but it was friendly and upbeat. Then, a few weeks later, Win called and said he wanted to come by again. I was not opposed to the idea, but I was beginning to feel as if every time I opened the door, I saw another Lewis come in. I did not know what this was about.

This time, he said that when I was running for bishop, he had said to Cathy that if I was elected, he was going to apply to be my administrative assistant. I was the kind of person he wanted to work under at that time in his life. Since I was not elected but was called to Christ and St. Luke's instead, he wanted to know if I would consider hiring him as my Associate Rector. I about fell over. He was a superstar. I would have been happy to be his assistant. I explained to him some of the realities of this fragile church. There were those who thought it might be going out of business. Several years earlier, a nearby Presbyterian church had been turned into a restaurant. One wag called Christ and St. Luke's "Ghent's next restaurant." An elderly parishioner suggested one day in my adult class that it would make a lovely extension to the Chrysler Museum, a fine arts museum a few blocks down the street.

It took a courageous leap of faith for Win to offer himself to Christ and St. Luke's and me. I was sure I could not give him a pay raise over what he had been receiving in Hampton. He said that was okay; he understood and was willing to come on those terms. Win ranks up there with Jack Spong and Leslie Smith. They are the three finest professional colleagues I ever worked with in all my years in the ministry. I am grateful to say that I was blessed with superior assisting clergy brothers and sisters throughout my ministry, but Win stands above all others in my love, admiration, and respect. He was instrumental in saving my career, my marriage, and that church.

Within weeks of his arrival, he came into the office with some exciting news. He said that Charlie Davey, a highly esteemed Christian educator, might be available to join us on the staff. I did not know how to respond. Everyone who knew Charlie understood that she was the best in the business. However, Christ and St. Luke's was so poor that I was sure we could not manage to bring her onto our team. Win said, "Let me take her out to lunch and talk to her!" Win had great persuasive charms. He knew how to appeal to someone as extraordinary as Charlie Davey. He came back later in the day to announce that she would be joining our staff for something like eight hours a week, or one-fifth time. In essence, she would coordinate the pre-school programs and design and oversee the classes for elementary school children. At least for the short term, Win would be the coordinator for junior high and senior high youth, which made my daughter much happier.

THE MINISTRY OF CHRIST AND ST. LUKE'S

At that point, I made a conscious decision that I was going to build a substantially new congregation within the walls of that great building. That is, I would try not to alienate the people who were there, but I was going to seek to attract people from outside who could bring new energy and creativity to Christ and St. Luke's. In the fall of 1990, we were getting ready for our first vestry elections, when one young man, Gary Shook, announced that he wished to run. He then said something I had never heard before or have never heard since; he said that he had a campaign platform. His platform was that he wished to help Jim Sell attract new young adults into the church. I wanted a hug him. That was exactly the kind of focus I aspired to in that congregation. Happily, he won, as did other committed people who believed that the church had a future. As time went on, most of the members of the search committee ended up on the vestry and they were all great assets. With each future election, a few people with fresh ideas managed to get elected and change was filling the air.

GROWTH, GROWTH AND MORE GROWTH

Little by little, things began to turn around. In those days, it was still common for membership to be recognized by the annual visit of the Bishop, who would either confirm or receive new members.[46] Of course, we welcomed anyone anytime, anyway. We did not ask them if they were baptized or confirmed before we offered them communion. That is always between each individual and God. We invited everyone to join our classes, to participate in our programs, to pledge and to be as active as they wished. However, if people wanted that symbol of full life in the Episcopal Church, the route was through confirmation or reception. One year, we had sixty-three confirmations and receptions. The next year we had forty-eight. I still do not know of any church anywhere in contemporary times that had such a windfall.

When I was in Sparta, I used to do something that was a little bit of a gimmick. It succeeded more in the public relations value than in any real sense. When I saw a moving van parked at a home, I would run to the bakery and purchase a dozen cookies. Then I would stop by the house and welcome the new residents. The act was always a simple act of hospitality, but the reputation that I would chase moving vans the same way lawyers allegedly would chase ambulances made a point. I

---

[46] Basically Confirmation is for people who are baptized, who wished to "confirm the promises made on their behalf at baptism." Reception is for those who have been confirmed in another denomination and wish to be received into the Episcopal Church.

could not do the same thing in more urban Norfolk, but I tried to maintain that same spirit of purposefulness. The church was booming. Win and I made a strategic decision to divide the week into two halves. We would have several adult classes and two worship services on Sundays. Then, on Wednesday evenings, we would have worship, followed by dinner, followed by three or four more classes. We had a team of skilled teachers, such as Connie and Bill Jones, Mary and Richard Beauchamp, Jim and Blair Bickford, B.J. and Tim Taylor and others who were happy to join Win and me in various educational adventures. What can I say? We packed them in. The weak spot in the operation was Wednesday evening youth programs. We tried to have a kind of study hall, but that was not effective. Otherwise, we did amazingly well.

MUSIC

The music program had always been one of our strongest suits. However, our wonderful Casavant organ was falling apart. It had been built to Grover Oberle's specifications in the 1960s.[47] Once the budget dried up, all basic maintenance was deferred and the instrument began to suffer. But through all these hard times, Allen Shaffer began to build a choir that was first class. Like everyone else on the staff, he figured out how to jury-rig people and property; both the organ and his musicians were his concerns. He managed to cobble together strong volunteers with

---

[47] Grover Oberle was a nationally recognized organist and choirmaster living in Boston when the Rev. Peyton Williams recruited him for Christ and St. Luke's. One of the inducements Peyton offered was "any organ you want!" Grover is generally recognized as a godfather of great classical music in the greater Hampton Roads area.

minimally paid section leaders. Finally, something happened that can only be seen as providential. On one Christmas Eve, at the midnight service, when there were about seven hundred people in church, our organ died. Halfway through the service, we had to announce that the remainder of the service would be either spoken or accompanied by a piano. Maybe people were finally beginning to get the idea that we were living on the fragile edge in that church. We were going to have to begin to address some of our financial needs.

The vestry asked Allen to begin a process of investigating what steps we would need to take to bring our organ back up to its former glory. After consultation with two major companies, he proposed that the Canadian firm of Orgues Letourneau be commissioned to revoice the instrument, replace its leathers, build a new console, and add several more ranks. The price tag was $150,000. Before we could hardly explain the situation, a generous anonymous donor came to our rescue. When the work was completed, the newly renamed Casavant-Letourneau organ was hailed in the industry as the finest instrument for its space south of New York City.

Allen organized any number of special concerts and performances. The organ attracted some of the finest players in the world, making us a major venue for the annual Virginia Arts Festival. One of my favorite events that he put together was his annual service of Advent Lessons and Carols, where we invited leading citizens to read the lessons. It attracted hundreds of non-members.

A few years later, I gave Allen a choice: either he could become the full-time organist and choir director or he could stay part-time and hire an assistant. Since he was still a full professor at Norfolk State, he opted for the assistant. With that, wonderful Henry Faivre came on board. In this case, the sum of the parts was greater than the whole. Allen was now rocking and rolling with the finest music program in Hampton Roads!

Pastoral Ministry

A church can do all the right things to build up its attendance and its income, but if it does not attend to the needs of its parishioners, there is something hollow about it. Win and I both believed that every person who went into the hospital should be met at the door by one of his or her clergypersons. Many mornings at six o'clock, one of us would be in the admitting section of Sentara Norfolk General or any other regional hospital, awaiting the arrival of a parishioner. Other times, we would practically be following an ambulance into the emergency room after we received a late night call. Often, the only thing we needed to do was wish them well and have a prayer for the success of whatever procedure they were about to have. Other times, we would stay with the family through the long hours of surgery or recovery. We believed that it was important for us to wrap our spiritual arms of friendship around the patient and family until that time when both a healing and a cure took place.

Saying good-bye at the death of a parishioner was both an honor and a time of deep sadness. To be invited into that sacred space where life was being transformed from Earth to Heaven was an intimacy that I will always treasure. I have reflected many times on why I eventually moved on from Christ and St. Luke's. One of the biggest reasons was that I had increasing sorrow at watching some of the people I loved the most slip away into death. I had a reasonable reputation as a preacher, but I must admit that I especially respected the opportunity to preach at funerals. I called them my orations. In the old, more formal days of the Episcopal Church, the line about a funeral was "If you did not know the person when you came in, you still would not know who it was when you left." Funeral services were dispassionate, impersonal and safe. A stiff-upper-lip was enabled by this spiritual austerity. I was determined that the people we buried would be remembered as unique and wonderful children of God. I kept my orations short, but I always tried to say memorable things about the deceased. Because we were something of a community resource, with ample seating and great music, some of our largest attendances were at funerals. I recall having at least three where we had standing room only with over eight hundred worshipers.

As the church grew, it became important for us to expand our pastoral resources. Try as we might, Win and I could not do it all. So I had a conversation with Lee Ann Avery and Doug Weymouth about the possibility of them taking on a program called the Stephen Ministry. The Stephen Ministry is a non-denominational and theologically neutral Christian program of lay pastoral care. The three of us traveled to Florida for a week and undertook their extended leadership training. Lee Ann and Doug became the primary trainers. I went along so that I would understand how the process worked and could be an active participant in it. ("The Christmas Hymn" you will find at the end of this book was written there while I listened to the instructional lectures.). Lee Ann is a lifelong member of the church and has a good husband, five stunning adult children and a passel of grandchildren. She and her family are at the bedrock of the life of that congregation. Doug is an amazing man. A remodeler of homes and qualified home inspector, he was the first person to introduce Habitat for Humanity to us. With his organizational skills and his good-natured zeal, he recruited sizable teams of men and women in the congregation to build low-cost housing in Norfolk. But this was a new venture for him. He and Lee Ann would recruit people who would accept a full of year of training to become spiritual friends of people in the congregation who were in some kind of personal need. They chose carefully and trained thoroughly. As a result, we had a strong program. It was up to the clergy to identify perspective care receivers and to let Lee Ann and Doug match them with caregivers. Some of those relationships lasted for many months and ended up producing great interior healing.

By this time, many clergy had been forced to back away from one-on-one pastoral counseling, due to the dramatic increase in inappropriate sexual behavior by a few church people. About the only personal counseling I engaged in had to do with preparing for sacraments like marriage, baptism and burial. Instead something new and more consistent with whom we were as the church was taking its place. Spiritual direction was replacing the old psychological model that was popular in prior decades. A treasure in our midst that separated Christ and St. Luke's from almost every other church in the area was Sue Crommelin-Dell. Sue was a trained Jungian Analyst with extra training is spiritual direction. When people wanted to spend an extended period of time considering their prayer life, the art of meditation or their journey of faith, Sue would work with them in the privacy such holy concerns required.

THE POWER OF HEALING TOUCH

My support for the laying on of hands for healing was an evolving thing. It first started in Sparta at the midweek service. When I came to Norfolk, there was already a midweek healing service in place and I was happy to keep it going. The subject of laying hands on people is complex. Again, I think of my West Virginia roots and the excessive passion of certain faith healers who would shout, "Heal!" at the top of their lungs and then catch a poor, ailing worshiper off balance, gently knocking him or her over into the waiting arms of a lieutenant and declaring that person "slain in the spirit." We knew there was another way. When a person comes to a quiet place in the church and quietly whispers the need for a particular kind of prayer and the one designated to offer the prayer lays his hands on that person's head and privately articulates that deep need, the experience is like being in a confessional booth. It is an intimate, personal and holy moment. The demand for the laying on of hands for healing became so great that we began offering it at all the services on Sunday and throughout the week. If Win was the celebrant, I would be the healer and vice versa. As church attendance grew, its popularity did not abate! We could not handle the crowds alone.

After careful consultation, we invited a few people to become healers as well. This was a big step for me, because I was afraid that we could lose the intimacy of the moment with an inappropriate or overly zealous prayer. I decided that I would seek out people who were already in the healing professions: doctors, nurses, and other medical personnel. They were honored to be asked and did a great job. They also gave a certain kind of imprimatur to what we were doing. One of the superstars who came into the church about that time was Anne Brower. She was an internationally recognized radiologist who was on the faculty of Eastern Virginia Medical School (EVMS). Anne ended up getting ordained and writing a book on spiritual healing.[48] In due course, she became the facilitator and principal guru of this ministry.

By the time I left Christ and St. Luke's in 2005, we were having about six hundred people in church on a Sunday morning, and fifty or more of those were seeking the laying on of hands. We continued to broaden the pool of healers and would have four or five available on any given Sunday. I was careful to publish guidelines and have training sessions that explained what was appropriate so there was no misunderstanding about what we were doing. This was not about something awkward and embarrassing. It was about gentle private moments of spiritual connectivity. To emphasize the point, it was widely understood that the clergy or anyone else would never be informed by the healers of the contents of the requests. The healers were scrupulous in following those guidelines and the popularity of this ministry spoke for itself.

AN AMAZING PARISH STAFF

Our staff grew and changed as budget and demand warranted. After a few years, Betty Denniston announced that she was ready to retire. Jane Dembert was hired to be her successor. Jane ended up being our longest tenured support staff person. She

---

[48] *I Am Not Ready to Die Yet: Stories of Healing,* R. Brent and Company, Asheville, NC (2006).

eventually evolved into our financial secretary. When it came time to look for a parish administrator, I found Joyce Safford who had recently graduated from the parish administrator's program at Union Seminary in Richmond, Virginia. She was a pro and was great asset in the life of the church. Our receptionist was Frances Halcrow. Answering the phone and greeting visitors was an enormous job in those days and Frances did the task with sensitivity and good humor.

Not long after I arrived, the Dean of the Cathedral in Portland, Oregon, Bill Wagner, arrived in Norfolk to retire to the hometown of his wife, DeeDee. Bill offered his services for the next twenty years as a midweek early morning celebrant of the Eucharist and constant polestar to our ministry. Gordon Davis was also a retired clergyman on our staff. He had served in the Diocese of Virginia for most of his career. When he first retired, he and his wife moved over to the eastern shore of Virginia. I think they found that location a little isolated, so they moved to Norfolk and he was part of our team for many years. The Rt. Rev. O'Kelly Whitaker was a gift of immeasurable value. Kelly had been the Dean of the Cathedral in Orlando and then Bishop of Central New York. A classmate of Bishop Charles Vache, he and his wife, Betty, moved to Portsmouth in retirement. There is nothing like having your own in-house bishop. Kelly would bring his great depth of wisdom and experience into the conversation when we needed him. I always said he was "my bishop," in that I always knew I could learn how to be a better priest through him.

CHRISTIAN EDUCATION

The ministry of providing Christian formation and nurture to children and teens was fundamental to who we were at the church. From the time when we had no babies in the nursery and three or four children in the youth group, we added a few children here and there until we reached a point where we had a thriving program. It all began with Charlie Davey. A natural, warm, embracing woman who loved children, she began a little children's ministry that grew deeply and broadly. She started with a half dozen little ones, and by the time I left, she could have thirty or forty sitting in a circle, listening to her stories of God's love. She worked hard to recruit and train skilled teachers. She had been a consultant to Virginia Seminary in curriculum development and brought great expertise along with her passion.

Happily, our population of worshipers from junior high school age through college age also grew. For several years, Win oversaw the ministry to them, but as we continued to develop as a parish, we began looking for someone who could take ownership of that population. Just when we needed her the most, the vivacious Carrie Short arrived in our lives. An ex-cheerleader at the University of Miami, she was born for the job. She loved working with the youth and she was close enough to the early twenty-somethings to be able to connect with them well. Ministry to youth is hard because everyone involved has a notion about how it ought to be conducted. The clergy have a notion. The parents have a notion. The youth have a notion. Somehow, Carrie was able to connect a line through all of those stakeholders and build a program that worked beautifully.

I have already spoken about our wildly successful Wednesday evening programs for adults. Sunday morning always attracted a considerable crowd as well. I encouraged others to offer an alternative to my classes, such as a Bible or book study, but I usually reserved that nine o'clock teaching hour for myself. It was an opportunity for me to explore new subjects, hear the questions of the congregation, and engage in a long-term dialogue with them. We ventured into many areas. For example, it was there that I discovered the beauty of Celtic spirituality and the wisdom of people like Elaine Pagels and Henri Nouwen. I hosted those conversations for fifteen years and we never ran out of things to talk about.

The other adult education program I maintained for many years was a Wednesday morning Bible study. That Bible study went on from 1990 until 2013, though it happened in different churches with different gatherings of students. I did have a surreptitious agenda. For those twenty-three years, I read, studied, and considered scripture with a gathering of faith-filled people who enriched me year after year. I suspect I taught the Gospel according St. John about six times. One of my favorite lessons was on the strange Revelation of St. John the Divine. Other than dreadful Leviticus, few books of the Bible were left out of that long-running experience. I have lost count of how many times I have read the Bible. I once tried to count and estimated it was twenty-seven times, but I am sure it could not have been that often![49]

STEWARDSHIP

Christ and St. Luke's was not a poor church. That is to say, most of the people had incomes and lived comfortably. But I did not seem to be successful in offering effective, imaginative leadership for stewardship. It was part of the lore of Norfolk that people are not generous in that city. One older parishioner lamented that as a young man in the 1960s, he was embarrassed by how little that church had paid its rector at the time. Except for that one comment, I cannot say whether that was true or not. But I do know that we had trouble developing a strong stewardship program. This is not to say that our budget did not increase. It did. However, in the fifteen years that I was there, our average attendance quadrupled, but our budget only tripled; not shabby, but not gaudy either! When I came there, I was not sure there was anyone who tithed. My attitude was that giving was an honor and giving to one's church was at the heart of a life lived as a Christian person. When we were educating children, it was hard for Ellen and me to tithe. But in the latter years, our needs were fewer, and we were able to join those who did. For the record, the church always lived within its means. I made sure of that. I was tight-fisted and never proposed a

---

[49] It all depends on how I choose to count. In the Episcopal Church, we read the Bible through in Sunday morning worship every three years. Since I studied those lessons each week to prepare for our services, that would be about seventeen times. Add to that about four or five times in my Bible study classes and another three or four times in personal study and I approach that total.

deficient budget. But there were many years when we could not squeeze out raises for any of the staff, despite the increasing demands being made on them.

OUTREACH

From my perspective, a goal of a rector of a church should be to encourage every single man, woman, and child to find a way to be directly involved in the life of at least one needy person. We have gone a long way from writing checks to nonprofit organizations and thinking we are doing good works. I learned from my camp administrator days in the Diocese of Newark that breaking down the walls of race, culture and clan happens best when we get to know one another personally and honestly. Today, outreach ministry is about broadening our personal involvement with people who are somehow different from us. Wonderful St. Matthew has Jesus say that, "Just as you did to the least of these who are members of my family, you did it to me." In other words, if you wish to see the face of Christ, stand at in a soup kitchen handing out slices of bread!

Christ and St. Luke's had some extraordinary programs. When I first came, Laura Blaylock and some other members began a Christmas program of angel trees. She contacted the city schools and they helped her identify children who would not have Christmas presents. Shopping lists were attached to a tree and parish families selected the one they wished to purchase. Then she created dozens of enormous "Santa Sacks" that members filled with the gifts the children had requested. A couple of Sundays before Christmas, we would drag those piles of sacks into church where we would bless them. Some might have thought it was pretentious, but I found it beautiful. Then Laura would coordinate their distribution.

Another early outreach began when I was at a meeting of Ghent clergy and we began to ask the question about how homeless people were managing to find meals in our neighborhood. With little effort, we all assigned our churches a day a week to provide lunch. I claimed Thursday because we were having Wednesday night parish dinners every week, and I knew there would be leftovers from those dinners. My earliest memory was that Sally Tobin offered to coordinate our lunches. She had a smart idea. Her husband, Jake, was the Admiral in charge of the Norfolk Naval base. They lived in naval housing in a section known as Admiral's Row. It was expected that high ranking officers should do a considerable bit of entertaining. Every week, somebody seemed to be having a dinner party on Admiral's Row, and the next morning, Sally would be at their kitchen door, looking for leftovers for our soup kitchen. No one was going to turn down Admiral Tobin's wife, and happily, no one wanted to! As time moved on, others jumped into this ministry, and it became a long-standing outreach program of the church.

A year or so later, Sally got another great idea. She had us join forces with members of Park Place United Methodist Church to begin tutoring elementary school children after school. They called it the Homework Club. We must have had twenty volunteers and the Methodist Church had another twenty or so. Twice a week, tutors would meet with their assigned students at the Methodist church to help with the homework. Of course, we offered bribes of cookies and other treats to the young scholars.

Right after that, yet another need was identified. It was clear that on cold nights, many homeless people had nowhere to get out of the weather. In 1992, the Unitarian church began inviting homeless people to sleep in their parish hall. They gave them dinner and a mattress for the night and breakfast the next morning. Although they did it all winter long by themselves, Christ and St. Luke's jumped in on about a half dozen nights when they needed a break. The following year, we split the program with the Unitarians. One week, we would keep the people; the next week, they would. It was exhausting. For about seven different weeks, we had sixty to eighty men and women sleeping in our building. We would fix them dinner, stay up through the night while they slept, and give them breakfast in the morning. I can recall times when they would be sleeping on our pews and dining on long tables down the center aisle of the church. That summer, the Unitarians and Episcopalians negotiated the creation of something called the Norfolk Emergency Shelter Team (NEST). A number of other local churches each took one or two weeks. The year after that, we grew to a point where a large number of congregations joined in and we only had to take one week a winter. We always opted for the week over New Year's Eve because a number of our members had that week off and were able to participate.

One of the most unique human beings I ever knew was the Rev. Dr. Michael Musolf. Michael grew up in Oregon and graduated from Pomona College with a major in physics. From there, he was accepted to the doctoral program in particle physics at Princeton University. His specialty was strange quarks. He then went to the Massachusetts Institute of Technology and did postdoctoral research. While he was there, he also became a student at the Episcopal Divinity School in Cambridge. He was ordained and arrived unexpectedly on our doorstep. He had taken a position as a professor of physics at Old Dominion University and was doing research at the electron accelerator, known today as Jefferson Labs, at Langley Air Force Base in Newport News. He said he was interested in working with inner-city boys and wanted to know if we could use him in some non-stipendiary ministry. I thought, *Are you kidding?* It was like someone giving us a huge, valuable, rare gift. He went over to Park Place and began playing basketball with some of the local boys. You have to understand that Michael was a thirty-something white man who was showing up to play basketball with some of the most difficult inner-city boys in our community. I do not know exactly how he did it, but he was a huge success. The next thing I knew, he was bringing them to church and introducing them to the congregation. He explained that he would love to have some help developing a ministry to these boys and he was surrounded by volunteers. We found it interesting that the predominately African-American churches in the Park Place community did not want them around. They were troublemakers and made their members uncomfortable. They could be unruly, confrontational and tough. Most of that first group of boys ended up doing time. Because we surrounded them with both love and gentle firmness, we never had any real problems. As time moved on, Michael and his team of volunteers created a program called "The Mission of the Holy Spirit". It was housed in various locations and served both boys and girls and their families. When Michael finally moved on to Pasadena and Caltech, Keith Josey took over and he has been its guiding light ever since.

THE LOST BOYS

I think I can say with due respect for all of our outreach programs that the one I held in highest regard was our ministry to those young men known as the "Lost Boys". The lost boys were a group of some twenty thousand six to eight year old Christian Dinka tribe boys who were living in southern Sudan when the northern Islamic military swarmed in during the early 1980s, killed their parents and took their sisters into slavery. For the next six years, they walked from Sudan to Ethiopia to Kenya before they could be housed in a UN refugee camp. By my estimate, the journey would be about the equivalent of walking from Norfolk to Boston and back to New York. Many of them died on the way. Some were eaten by crocodiles or lions or accidentally ate poisonous food. Others were killed by the military and rebel tribesmen. They stayed in the refugee camp for years until about 1996, when Church World Service began placing them among American churches for resettlement. None of them knew how old he was, although they probably ranged from between nineteen to twenty-two. They all declared January 1 to be their birthdate. They were spread all over America and made considerable national news when they arrived. A sizable percentage of them were raised as Episcopalians. We were contacted and agreed to accept five of them. Other Norfolk churches took some and still more were placed in Newport News. I cannot remember all of their names but Deng Awuou and John Lueth stand out. They both remain actively involved at Christ and St. Luke's

Initially, Anna Noon took responsibility for getting some people together to find them an apartment, furniture, and other necessities. Then we had to find them jobs and get them into school. During one of their first days among us, I had the pleasure of taking them shopping for clothes and out to lunch. They had had no experience with Western culture. Before arriving in America, they had never been in a car or seen a light bulb or a pane of glass. When I told them that they could not be real Americans until they went to McDonald's, they did not know what McDonald's was, but they were ready to learn. Then I said they needed to order Big Macs. They had never had any kind of sandwich, but when I told them it contained beef, they all said, "We like beef!" They had been cattle herders and knew beef. The Big Macs came and they did not know how to eat them. Eating with their fingers was something they were not used to. It was considered bad form in the Dinka world. Finally, Deng picked his up and tried to stuff the whole thing in his mouth. He got special sauce all over his face. The other boys howled in delight, but finally, they got the hang of it and loved this new treat.

Eventually, Kelly Wood became almost like their father. He took it upon himself to help them find work and take basic GED education classes. John finished college at Old Dominion University. Maybe others of them did as well. Some went to Tidewater Community College. They were bright young men. On my last Sunday at Christ and St. Luke's, they and a large number of other local lost boys came and did a going away ceremonial dance in my honor. I well up thinking of that moment.

ENDOWMENT

Christ and St. Luke's had about $1.5 million in endowment when I arrived. It grew to about $2.5 million when I left. There had been no endowment program up until the 1960s, even though the church was nearly three hundred years old at the time. An active attorney, Harry McCoy, had set up an endowment process, and some assets began to come into it, mostly by will and estate planning.

We established an estate program called the A. Heath Light Society, named after the Bishop of Southwest Virginia, who had been rector in the 1970s. Members were given a small lighthouse lapel pin as a symbol of their support. While we were able to encourage a number of people to remember Christ and St. Luke's, most of them stayed happily alive, and those assets were slow to come in. The endowment was managed by NationsBank, later called Bank of America. Cy Grandy, a parishioner, represented the bank and did a good job of managing our assets. However, we also had an endowment committee. It was chaired by Charles Tucker. George Curtis and Bryant McGann were also on the committee at the time I left. I was invited to come to the meetings and I decided right there that it was time I learned something about trusts and endowments. If we were going to have a struggling stewardship program, it would have to be offset by other income streams. Charles was the managing partner of a prominent Norfolk law firm. George was the recently retired executive of a ship repair company and Bryant was a bright young attorney. It was a great team. I was supposed to get the vestry to elect someone new every four years, but they were so good that I managed to "forget" when someone's term was up. Besides, in this instance, a long view and skilled training superseded political correctness in my eye. All I did was sit there, ask questions, and learn as much as I could.

The Consortium of Endowed Episcopal Parishes

After a year or so, it dawned on me that we were eligible to join the Consortium of Endowed Episcopal Parishes (CEEP), the most sophisticated continuing education program for parishes in America. To be a member, a church has to have at least one million dollars of endowment, but the dues are steep and the cost of attending their annual conference is high. There was no way the budget of the parish could support our membership, so I proposed that it be a cost of managing the endowment, just like our fees to NationsBank. The endowment committee went along with the plan and made it possible for me and a few other parishioners to attend on a regular basis. Actually, I used my continuing education fund for my expenses. Ellen often attended with me at our own personal expense. She ended up becoming a skilled consultant to clergy in financial planning. Virginia Theological Seminary brings her to its campus each year to guide older alumni in their retirement preparation. I cannot begin to explain how much we learned at those annual conferences. I learned the smart way to manage endowments and the shrewd way to spend assets. I also learned creative ways to develop outreach and the newest ways to engage the principalities and powers the church always has to come up against. Each conference had major speakers from all over the world who spoke about the future of Christianity and our impact upon civilization. Bill Moyers, Desmond Tutu, and Ray Suarez stand out. We went to places like Indianapolis, San Francisco, New York, Atlanta, and New Orleans. In every city, we saw all the greatness of the Episcopal Church and my vision

of us as a denomination was continually strengthened. This was
my principal continuing education through these years and it
gave me a worldview of the Anglican Church and all religions
that held me in good stead throughout my career.

NUDGEES

While I was there, Christ and St. Luke's became something of
a case study for the development of parish ministry. That is,
by all the external norms of success, we were seen as a vibrant
congregation and that stimulated people's curiosity. A number
of parishioners came to me to express an interest in ordination.
In a parallel way, I thought it was part of my job to raise the
possibility of the ordained ministry as an option for certain
people whom I personally identified. Before I came to Norfolk,
two people - Betsy Walker, whom I mentioned earlier, in West
Virginia and Bill Gandenberger in New Jersey - both found
their way into the ordained ministry. Once I was in Norfolk, I
was flooded by a tide of prospective clergy. On three different
occasions, I created long-term conversations with six to eight
individuals at a time who wanted to explore the ministry. I
called them our "nudgees;" they were individuals who seemed
to be in the midst of being nudged into the ministry by the
Holy Spirit. Usually joined in these conversations by one of
my assistants, we discussed all of the joys and hard times of
ministry. When I could bring in examples of my failures, I did.
When I could articulate the deep satisfactions I received, I did
that as well.

Of course, most of them did not go that route, but we ended
up with eleven Episcopal clergypersons coming out of Christ
and St. Luke's. The former President and Dean of the Virginia

Theological Seminary, Martha Horne, once told me that at that time, Christ's and St. Luke's was second in the nation among all Episcopal churches for sending people to seminary. I am not sure how she knew that, because our students went to a variety of institutions and several achieved their goals by a kind of cobbled together education. In my fifteen years, these people all ended up as ordained Episcopal clergy: Julia Tucker, Connie Jones, Ann Brower, Sue Crommelin-Dell, Anna Noon, Mary Garner, Jim Puryear, Connie Jackson, Lauren McDonald, Sarah Odderstol, and Valerie Hayes.

As I write this, I can say with joy and thanksgiving that each of them has been a gift to the church and served with distinction and deep effectiveness. When I think about what kind of legacy I leave the Episcopal Church, I think of these clergy. To put a fine edge on these numbers, I would add Joe Rushton in Severna Park, Hank Bristol in Princeton, and Catherine Amon (who, sadly, died before she could complete the process) in New Haven. Then there is Llyn Lantz, who became a Lutheran Pastor and Derrick Turietta, an ordained Roman Catholic Deacon. These eighteen clergypersons have brought great wisdom, depth of knowledge and faithfulness to thousands of people. The whole church has been enriched by them all.

AFTER WIN

As you read this, you might begin to think that Win and I were married. I hardly did anything without his approval and he was constantly consulting me. But he was way too good to always be somebody's associate. So finally, in 1998, he accepted a call to be the Rector of Old Donation Episcopal Church in Virginia Beach. It was a great fit. An old church was a rich history, he launched a growth spurt there that would go on for many years into the future. I remember being invited to preach the sermon at his installation. I said something that was meant to sound like a money back guarantee. I said, "If you are not completely satisfied with this product, you may wrap him back up in the accompanying cassock and ship him back to his original destination, because we will always take Win Lewis back." I could not have guessed that some ten years later, Win would return to Christ and St. Luke's for a third time as the Rector. This man's heart and soul are woven into the fabric of that church.

By that time, I did not have to cringe and fret when it came to looking for a new assistant. After only ten years, we had become a nationally recognized parish. We were in a position to be competitive in recruiting new clergy. I was talking to Angelica Light one day shortly after her arrival from Roanoke and she told me about the Assistant Rector at her former church, Lottie Cochran. Angelica was high on Lottie and I was high on Angelica. Angelica's recommendation carried enormous weight with me. She said that Lottie had grown up in Norfolk and was hoping a time might come when she could return to her roots. I called her right away. I was so impressed that I practically offered her a job over the phone. Of course, we needed to go through all the standard procedures. She came and did a great job for us for about two years.

Lottie's shining moment was a time of great national tragedy. It was the day the airplanes flew into the World Trade Center, the Pentagon, and Pennsylvania farmland on September 11, 2001. In less than two hours, Lottie had organized a noon-time service of grieving and prayer, communicated its availability to both the congregation and the wider community and saw that the necessary details were put in place. It was the first service in the Hampton Roads area. We had perhaps three hundred people in the congregation. Most of them were not members of the church. Many came from the medical complex down our street. The press was there. A photograph of me standing in the pulpit in tears was picked up by the AP and published around America. What I remember most about that service was that we offered the laying on of hands for healing to everyone who wished it. That impromptu congregation of mostly non-Episcopalians poured out of their pews and came forward for that blessing. I never saw anything like it! Then Lottie organized an equally effective service for the early evening of the same day and a very large one on the following Sunday.

Lottie did great work, but shortly after she arrived, she adopted two little girls from Russia. They were a blessed handful, so after a while, she did the wise thing and went off to become a full-time mommy until such a time as she could re-enter the parish ministry.

After Lottie, Gary Manning popped into our church right out of seminary. An old friend once asked me how I always managed to get such great staff members. It was not hard. I could tell in minutes whether a person had the right stuff. I snapped Gary up as fast as I could. Not an off-the-shelf Episcopalian, he had been raised in the Assemblies of God, perhaps the most fundamentalist Christian denomination in America - real southern revivalism. When he was in high school in Florida, he was ordained to be an itinerant preacher. He did that for a while, until one day, he thought he would like to go to college. His colleagues said to him that going to college would be a mistake because higher education would hinder the flow of the Holy Spirit. After due deliberation, he decided he was going to go to college anyway. His old colleagues were correct. He was a brilliant student, and even though he went to an Assemblies of God college, he was no longer comfortable in that revivalist spirituality. He took a secular position for a few years. By that time, he was living in Richmond. On Christmas Eve, 1989, some friends invited Gary and his wife to the Midnight Service at their Episcopal church and he was converted to our denomination that night. When he went to Virginia Seminary and took his first test in the introductory New Testament course, his professor called him in and said, "Why are you in this class?" I think she had never had a student as brilliant as Gary. But that was only part of who Gary was. He was funny and charming and a man of deep faith. The long and the short of it was that Gary was not with us long. When he was in Alexandria, he worked in a church where the rector became a bishop in Wisconsin. The first person that bishop recruited to build up his diocese was Gary Manning. Frankly, I would have done the same thing.

After Gary had been there one year, it became clear that we could indeed use two assistant rectors. The Rev. Dr. Connie Jones had been on my search committee; she was the Senior Warden and an active member of the church. Trained as a historian and married to a political scientist, Connie taught at Tidewater Community College and Bill, her husband, taught at Virginia Wesleyan College. Connie had wanted to be a priest since her childhood. She was one of those women who knew throughout her life that she had been called to the ministry. However, once the door opened to women, she was enmeshed in all the duties of motherhood and career. Finally, she was able to put together a theological education by attending a year at Virginia Seminary and a year at Union, the Presbyterian seminary in Richmond, and engaging in independent study. This was a woman with a Ph.D. from Duke University. She was completely capable of studying effectively on her own.

Some might have thought that it was a bad idea for me to call Connie Jones to be my assistant along with Gary Manning. All the experts will say that you never hire anyone, either lay or ordained, from within the congregation. But Connie was a good idea. She had a home in the area, her husband was settled in his job, and their children were either in college or graduate school. I knew Connie, she knew me, and our relationship was fabulous. I could not perceive that within a year or so after she was hired and Gary had moved on, I would announce my retirement and leave her in an awkward position. Despite her maturity and experience, I needed to be there for her, and I was not. She went through a hard time for a while, as her beloved husband, Bill, slipped into heaven because of a brain tumor. After I left, she finally ended up on her feet at Grace Church, Yorktown.

CHAPTER 8

TWO TURNING POINTS

If we study the ebb and flow of attendance in the American Episcopal Church, we will see that there was steady growth from the beginning of the twentieth century until the mid-1960s. Then, slowly, there was a downward turn that continued until about 1990. For the next ten years after that, there was something of an upswing. It seemed to be after the revision of the Prayer Book and the general acceptance of the ordination of women and gay persons. Those were the years when I was at Christ and St. Luke's and we benefited greatly. Then something happened; something that I fully approved of and believed we were made far better as a denomination because of. In 2003, the General Convention of the Episcopal Church gave its consent for the consecration of Gene Robinson as Bishop of New Hampshire. Gene Robinson was the first openly gay man to be consecrated a bishop. His diocese knew who he was; there was never any attempt to gloss over his orientation. He was fully qualified and a completely appropriate choice. but the national conservative secular press had a field day. Right-wing fundamentalist denominations screamed at us and called us every name in the book. I thought the heat from ordaining women and revising the Prayer Book was bad. This upheaval was like a torch lit under us. In a talk I heard Bishop Robinson give at Princeton, someone asked why he thought the fire and brimstone that followed his election was so much worse than that which transpired following the other controversies. He made the point that the increased use of computers through e-mail, blogs, and social media networks gave angry people more venues to express themselves. That made sense. All I know is that in Christ and St. Luke's, all growth stopped. We had trouble attracting new worshipers going forward. Philosophically, our church took the high moral ground. I was proud of our intelligence, courage and compassion. I was not so captivated by numbers that I would ever raise even a hint of anxiety, but facts are facts; the days of sixty-three member confirmation classes came to a grinding halt. The problem became systemic. Many bishops quietly stopped going to churches for confirmation services. They saw the handwriting on the wall and discreetly opted for regional confirmations, which were inconvenient, tedious and attracted almost no one. The chief public function of a bishop is to be a communicator and advocate for his or her churches. It is through them alone that the hope and the vision of the diocese are generated. Bishops are always expected to be the preachers at any services they are participating in. By the early years of the new millennium, I even heard of bishops who tried to find ways not to preach at confirmation services. I think they were too demoralized by the public reaction they observed. They were going to be attacked no matter what position they took.

The second turning point was within our own congregation. We were bursting at the seams. We did not have room for another Sunday school class or another outreach program. To make matters worse, many of our spaces were unusable. At very high tides, our nursery would fill up with water. There was an old residence attached to the church that was a serious firetrap with massive termite infestation. The building erected as a temporary structure after World War II as a parish hall was substandard in every other way. There had been conversations for years about what to do. In my travels around to other resource-sized churches[50] in metropolitan areas similar to ours, I saw that there was at least one Episcopal church that centered itself in the heart of the community and served a wider audience than just the congregation. It was not necessarily the designated Cathedral, but it did take on that kind of civic identity. We had a major medical complex two blocks in one direction and an opera house and world-class museum in another direction. We were sitting on a broad boulevard-like street overlooking an inlet of the Elizabeth River. We had a stunning church building. I said to everyone who asked that we needed to be the emblematic standard bearer for matters of faith in South Hampton Roads. My, did I not sound grandiose? People said they agreed, but they probably had their unarticulated doubts.

In order to achieve the kind of central focus I believed we should seek to attain, I argued that we needed to erect an

---

[50] In church sociology, there are four different parish sizes. If attendance averages 0–50 per Sunday, the parish is called a family-sized church. A parish of 51–150 is pastoral sized. A parish of 151–400 is program sized. A parish that averages more than 400 on a Sunday is resource sized. Within each category, a definable life and ministry gets played out in very concrete ways. There are substantial dislocations within the parish culture when a new category is established. Christ and St. Luke's leaped from pastoral size to resource size between 1990 and 1994. Some experts would say we grew too fast. It takes most congregations a decade to adjust to just one of these transformations. Skipping from pastoral size to resource size caused a kind of new reality some people could never adjust to.

addition that would be an instant part of the architectural tour of Norfolk. I then made the point that perhaps the greatest architect to ever come out of Virginia since Thomas Jefferson was a man who spent his childhood at Christ and St. Luke's. His name is Barton Myers. He lives in Santa Barbara, California and he is considered one of the top architects in America. My notion was that we could have Barton create an addition to our church that would be elegant, functional and a work of art, as our church building is, but within a twenty-first century idiom. With such a building, we could transform our ministry in a dramatic way.

The vestry discussed this idea thoroughly and created a committee of bright, visionary people chaired by Guil Ware and co-chaired by Jim Bickford and George Compo to begin a formal exploration. When the time was right, we invited Barton to Norfolk and asked him to envision a space that would fit on our property and fill our program needs. He came up with a fabulous plan; in retrospect, it was probably too fabulous.

Barton called for removing the old house and the parish hall and replacing them with an open atrium area that would be flexible enough for many different program needs. When we presented the idea to the congregation, there was excitement but hesitation. This was going to be a multimillion-dollar project, and there were a lot of questions about whether that kind of money could be raised in Norfolk. As our committee thought about it, we identified four or five families who had the capacity to make substantial gifts to the campaign, should we go forward. We then selected a fund-raising group to help us through the process. They did all the proper research and said that it would be a stretch for us but it could be doable if we received some of those major lead gifts.

As we began the campaign, the Ghent Neighborhood League rose up in opposition. They were convinced that we were going to change the fundamental nature of the neighborhood with this building. Over and over again, we assured them that we sought to be good neighbors, but they would not back off. They sued us three times. In every instance, they lost, but the cost of defending ourselves ate up much of the income our campaign raised. And naturally, the families who could have made the project happen did not wish to be identified with such a controversial proposal.

In our effort to get along with the Ghent Neighborhood League, we even took down the old residence and ten apartments we also owned. All we accomplished by doing that was to lessen our assets even more.

I now know that I misread the tea leaves. Christ and St. Luke's was so far out in front of national norms that we did not see what the general climate of church life really was. Unbeknownst to us, construction of new churches had ground to a halt across America. Most dioceses cannot remember when the last major new church building project took place. Even major additions are rare in this era of closing churches.

After three or four years of constant renegotiation, lawsuits and deep distress, the whole project was put on the shelf. All I could think of was that if I had known it was going to turn out that way, I would have never begun. The ordeal exhausted me. At age sixty-three, I felt I had nothing left to offer these people, and rather than drag them into a less-energized era, I determined that it was time for me to retire and let them find someone with fresh zeal and drive. That church was a constant sixty hour a week operation for the rector and, after fifteen years, I could not keep up that pace any more.

RETIRING THE FIRST TIME

In May 2005, I retired from Christ and St. Luke's. Angelica and Henry Light coordinated a two-day retirement celebration that included old colleagues who came to town and offered testimonials. I felt as if I was attending my own funeral, and it was fabulous. I preached my last sermons, celebrated my last Eucharists, and took off for a month to a condo in the PGA Golf Village in Port St. Lucie, Florida, that dear friends Lee Georges and Lois Kercher let me use, where I wrote some three hundred thank-you notes and played golf till I was tired of the game.

I love Christ and St. Luke's beyond description. What began as "Ghent's next restaurant" evolved into a broad-based Episcopal church that brought worshipers from as far south as the North Carolina border, as far north as Williamsburg, as far west as Smithfield and as far east as the oceanfront of Virginia Beach. The greatest professional honor of my life was to be its rector. Despite the hard knocks of the last three years or so, wonderful things were accomplished. We proved over and over again that parish life will soar even in this era of secularization when worship is beautiful, preaching enters the soul and the program life is personally involving.

MEANWHILE, BACK AT HOME

I am scrolling back to 1991. After we arrived in Norfolk, Katie attended the eighth grade at Norfolk Academy, but the school did not fit her personality, so she transferred to Maury High School the next year. Taking a clue from her brother, she began having a conversation about boarding school. We had no problem with that, but our lives were in such disarray that it was hard for us to give the matter the kind of attention it required. She started to consider the Lawrenceville School in Lawrenceville, New Jersey. Going back to New Jersey carried a certain appeal for her. When Ellen and I could not find a way to get her to her interview, we did the unorthodox thing of having Andrew drive her up when he was home. I wonder what the school officials thought. Some of the students who come to Lawrenceville for interviews arrive in expensive cars with parents carefully in tow. Here was a little girl with her big brother knocking at the door for admission. She had done well on her Secondary School Aptitude Tests and presented herself beautifully. However, she was placed on the waiting list, so she returned to Maury High School for a second year. The next time she applied to boarding schools, we were far more settled and could give the topic the kind of attention she deserved. She and Ellen drove up through New England, northern Virginia, and New Jersey and looked at a number of schools. She was accepted to four schools. She took Choate off the list because it was too far from home. Exeter, in New Hampshire, was even farther away, but they offered her a generous scholarship. This time, Lawrenceville let her in and offered her some scholarship aid, but it was not as generous as Exeter's offer. On admission day, Ellen called Lawrenceville and said that Katie wanted to come there but that Exeter had offered her much more money. They asked how much more. When Ellen told them, they simply said, "Okay, we will match it." It was not a free ride, but it was enough!

So Katie spent her last two years at wonderful Lawrenceville School. The headmaster was a man named Si Bunting, who was well known in Virginia academic circles because he had been president of both Hampton-Sydney College and, later, the Virginia Military Institute. He and Katie hit it off well. She joined him on a summer adventure through the West and they spent a lot of time getting to know one another. Early on in her senior year, as they were talking, he asked her where she wanted to go to college. She expressed interest in several schools, but she was particularly interested in the College of William and Mary. He said that he had a friend there who might be of some influence and asked if she would like for him to write to his friend. Katie, of course, said yes. It turned out that the President of William and Mary was the friend Si Bunting had in mind, and she was accepted. It did not hurt that Katie was completely qualified anyway.

Katie spent four years at William and Mary, majoring in anthropology. Beside the fact that it is a superior school (currently ranked the number-one public university for teaching by *US News and World Report*), I think she liked being close to home. She has always been closely bonded to her mother and had missed Ellen when she was at Lawrenceville. We made a deal with her that we would never travel into Williamsburg without her full knowledge. She rarely washed her own clothes while she was there. She bought a lot of the college-girl basics and came home often enough that her mom made sure her clothes were clean. She did well in that academically challenging environment. Anthropology turned out to be exactly the right major for her.

OUR TWO YOUNG ADULTS

Andrew graduated from Georgetown in 1994. He had a wonderful time there majoring in international relations. He spent part of his junior year in Chile. Both of our children became fully bilingual in English and Spanish. During his senior year, he lived in a house in Georgetown with five other guys. They became lifetime friends. To this day, he is in contact with many of them on practically a daily basis (love that Facebook!). His first summer out of college, he worked in the kitchen of a country club on Cape Cod. Next, he took a job in Boston, recruiting teenagers for the Job Corps for a couple of years. Most of his work there required that he speak Spanish. Then he was hired by a start-up firm in Charlottesville to develop business in China. He did that for three or four years. During that time, he became a world citizen and got to know his way around China well, keeping an apartment in Beijing. While he was living in Charlottesville, a mutual friend introduced him to a young med student at the Medical College of Virginia in Richmond. Her name is Neelam. Born of Indian parents in New Jersey, Neelam was a recent graduate of Duke University. She is charming, vivacious, and off-the-wall brilliant. She told us that her long-term career objective was to establish a clinic for multiply handicapped youth. What was there not to love about this young woman? Thus began their courtship.

Meanwhile, in her senior year of college, Katie determined that she wished to become a Peace Corps volunteer. Her uncle Bob had been one many years earlier. The College of William and Mary has a great track record of sending people into the program. Katie's Spanish was excellent. She was born to do this! After applying and being accepted, she was trained and sent to El Salvador in 1999. I had not seen living conditions like hers since I left Avondale hollow in West Virginia in the 1960s. Assigned to a village high up in the mountains, she lived in one room of a building that was attached to a pigsty. She shared a toilet with about fifteen other people. Although it flushed, it required a bucket of water poured in to make it work. She started a library, introduced beekeeping and organized tree planting projects. Many Peace Corps volunteers will tell you that it is one of the defining experiences of their lives. I am sure Katie would confirm that. Parenthetically, I think it is interesting that about thirty-five years earlier, I had thought I might work for either the Job Corps or the Peace Corps. Nothing came of that, but the next generation of Sells lived out both of those experiences.

Normally, the Peace Corps is a two-year assignment. Many of the volunteers never make it that long, as they wear out and go home early. Katie found a life in the Peace Corps and ended up staying a third year as a volunteer coordinator under the Director for Peace Corps in El Salvador.

Scrolling Back One More Time

In 1956, Ellen's brother, Bob, left their home in Pittsburgh for his freshman year in college. From then on, her family began to travel different journeys. It would have been somewhat amazing if, just before he went away, they had sat around a table and said, "Okay, in about thirty-five years, we are all going to reconvene in Norfolk, Virginia." Of course, that conversation did not happen, but the reconvening did. You already know Ellen's saga. Bob married a couple of years after us. His wife, Jean

Armour Major, graduated from Lake Forest College and earned
a Ph.D. in library science from the University of Illinois. She
was an academic librarian who ended up serving universities in
seven states. Bob became a mineral economist and worked in
eleven states. Ellen's parents, Bill and Mac Major ("Daddy Bill"
and "Granny Mac"), eventually retired to Mac's hometown of
Murray, Kentucky. After living there for a number of years,
they moved to a retirement community in Fort Myers, Florida.
After a fairly short period of time, Bill died, and Mac began
exhibiting symptoms of Alzheimer's disease. Bob and Ellen
kept her there as long as they could, with the help of caregivers.

In 1990, we moved to Norfolk. A couple of years later,
Jean accepted the position of Head Librarian at Old Dominion
University. She had been in a similar position at Ole Miss, so
when the ODU position opened up, she was a prime candidate.
Their careers had often taken them to different locations, but
on the weekends, they would usually fly to some mutually
accessible city to be together. When Bob began a process that
led to retirement, they made a decision to relocate together to
Norfolk. After some consultation, Bob and Ellen elected to
bring their mother up from Florida to a nursing home in the
Ghent neighborhood of Norfolk. There we all were, gathered
as if we were natives. Only Daddy Bill was missing.

In an odd little twist of history, Ellen has postcards her
mother wrote when she was traveling with Procter and Gamble.
Several of those postcards were written from Ghent Arms, a
hotel in Ghent. This was the same building she moved into from
Florida. While it kept its name, it had been converted into a
nursing home and assisted-living residence. Granny Mac was
there for quite a few years. Her condition was poor, but she had

a stout heart and nothing slowed her down. It was hard for us to visit with her because, by this time, she knew no one. We looked in on her about once a week just to make sure she was being well cared for. When she died, she joined Daddy Bill in the cemetery in Murray.

Jean had a great career at ODU that ended in retirement. By that time, Bob was active in a variety of volunteer activities. He helped people with their taxes, served as his Presbyterian church's treasurer, delivered blood for the Red Cross, and worked in a food-distribution center. Jean is an accomplished choir singer. Not only does she volunteer to sing in a variety of churches, but she is also active in the Virginia Symphony chorus.

One night in 2010, Bob got up to go to the bathroom. Unexpectedly, his blood pressure plummeted; he passed out and fell backward. As he fell, he hit his neck on the shower stall and fractured two vertebrae. He was taken to Norfolk General Hospital, where he was a patient for about two months. It was determined that he was a partial paraplegic; he could move his arms and fingers but not his thumbs and other lower body parts. He was on a respirator for a while and had a pacemaker inserted into his chest. Eventually, he was moved into a high tech wheelchair to begin his new life. He was transferred to the spinal injury clinic of the Medical College of Virginia in Richmond, where he underwent occupational and physical therapy for a couple more months. Jean received training as well so she would know how to manage his care. Before that time, they had moved from a house to a condominium in the Larchmont neighborhood, which was satisfactory for their needs. They have both become heroes to us. Bob has made a life for himself that is full and active. Using computers, e-mail, and all the technical wizardry that exists today, he stays current with his many interests. Jean has become Bob's primary caregiver. While they have nursing assistance on a regular basis, they share a full life of stimulating activities. When they chose to return to their beloved Chautauqua Institution in western New York in the summers, I knew that they were finally victorious over that ugly accident.

Lois and Lee

When we moved to West Ghent in 1990, we were slow to meet our neighbors. We had been used to the culture of New Jersey, where one did not necessarily bond with the people in his or her neighborhood. However, next door to us was a married couple whom we had seen come and go from time to time. They were about our age. His name is Lee Georges, and her name is Lois Kercher. Lee was a retired Navy doctor who had taken the position of Director of Eastern Virginia Medical School's newly created Diabetes Institutes. Lois was the Director of Nursing at Sentara Norfolk General Hospital. One day, Lois stopped Ellen and said that her stepson, Cam, was going to be married by Win at Christ and St. Luke's. Cam's bride was a personal friend of Cathy Lewis, so Win was happy to tie the knot. Ellen made the comment that we were going to be out of town but said they would be welcome to use our house for extra sleeping quarters for the large family delegation that was coming. That conversation was the start of a long and wonderful friendship for us.

We have done many things together. Lee and I both became members of the Greenbrier Country Club and have played hundreds of rounds of golf together. We chose Greenbrier because it was a club that accepts absolutely everyone who is willing to pay the dues. Neither of us could let ourselves be members of organizations that appeared to be exclusive and unwelcoming. To this day, Lee and I are pretty equal in our skill level. That makes playing together fun. We refuse to enter tournaments or determine handicaps. We play match play rather than stroke play, so when one of us wins a hole, the loser just picks up his ball, and we move on.

All of us are retired now. Lois got her doctorate in nursing and went on to be the Director of Nursing of the entire eleven hospital Sentara Health Care System. Lee made the Diabetes Institutes one of the premier facilities of its kind in the nation. He and I have now moved to the green tees, where the old men play. A good day in my life is beating him at golf. He would say the same thing about beating me!

TRAVELING THE WORLD

I have been to, I think, thirty-one foreign countries and forty-five states of the union. Ellen has been to a few more countries and states, because she has been with Katie to Africa and with friends to the U.S. northwest. Our travels together began when we got married and took off for England and France in 1970. So far, we have been to the British Isles six times and to France ten times. Our biggest venture abroad was in 1996, when Ellen and I both took sabbaticals and spent four months traveling around the world. One of our goals was to travel in the footsteps of St. Paul. We have been everywhere he traveled except his birthplace in Tarsus (now in south central Turkey) and Cyprus. We also wanted to experience the great religions of the world,

especially Islam, Buddhism and Hinduism. Ellen managed to
take a whole year away from teaching. In the fall, she planned
this journey and after Easter, we took off. Katie joined us in
Hong Kong, India, Thailand and Egypt.

We have had many other opportunities to travel as well.
We have been blessed by a friendship with wonderful Sylvia
Temmer and Bob Turoff, who had a pied-à-terre in Paris that
they allowed us to return to several times. A few years ago,
we went to Ireland and Paris with our friends Greg and Libby
Johnson. Libby is a little younger than we are. I asked her
to take on a particular duty, if she would. Every time I have
been to Paris, I have stopped at Le Deux Magots, a café in the
Saint-Germain-des-Prés area of the Left Bank. It is famous for
being a hangout of people like Jean Paul Sartre, Albert Camus,
Ernest Hemingway, Simone de Beauvoir and Pablo Picasso. I
know that I am nothing more than a tourist living in reflected
glory, but oh, how I love it. I asked Libby, if my children or
grandchildren could not, to take some of my cremated remains
to France and sprinkle them around there, perhaps even in the
flowerpots. I would know that my soul would linger in that
place forever. I also want her to pour some of my remains into
the Greenbrier River. My soul shall linger there as well. If I
ever get a hole-in-one, I want some near that place as well, just
like my old friend, Todd Ford arraigned. She agreed to this
strange request, although the bulk of our ashes will go into the
columbarium at Christ and St. Luke's.

When I was in high school, my wonderful French teacher,
Elsie Bolin, would say, "It is not if you get to Paris. It is when
you get to Paris." I used to say to myself that it was not going
to happen. People from West Virginia did not do things like

go to Paris. Because I married a woman who was far more
adventuresome than I knew how to be, I can say, *"Bonjour,*
Mademoiselle Bolin. Merci pour la langue française et pour
la vie belle en Paris!"

ENVIRONMENTAL THEOLOGY

As I said earlier, Ellen and I got to a point where we became
regular tithers. Once I stepped down from Christ and St. Luke's,
we began to have discussions about how to give some of our
resources away. At about that time, a seminary classmate and
good friend, Peter Kreitler, set up a fund at Virginia Seminary
to introduce environmental theology into the program life of
the school. This hit us as an important idea. Norfolk is the
second lowest eastern coastal town after New Orleans. On
top of that, the land mass we sit on is subsiding. We live right
across the street from the beautiful Elizabeth River, a tributary
of the Chesapeake Bay. We know that trouble is coming. Only
a cynic will say that the future of our environment will have
to be resolved by our children. All the issues of the twentieth
century will pale in comparison to the environmental mess
we are creating in the twenty-first century. There must be an
ethic of the environment that even the least enlightened of our
citizens can grasp. It is possible. In my lifetime, I have seen
the most intransigent people realize that smoking is insane,
seat belts save lives and junk food kills. We do change when
we have to! The church must be on the front end of this fight,
just as it has been in other arenas of cultural change, such
as race relations and gender equality. When it became clear
that the Kreitlers would accept gifts to support the program,
we chipped in with a fairly generous contribution. The VTS

Director of Development at the time, Ed Hall, consulted with Pete and together they proposed that Ellen and I set up our own fund - the James and Ellen Sell Environmental Scholarship Fund. With that money, the seminary is able to support students, faculty, or staff members who wish to do some kind of special training in environmental theology. The initial goal of an endowment to handle that kind of income was achieved and oversubscribed thanks to additional contributions from others, including generous gifts from Eastern Shore Chapel and Bob and Jean Major.

OUR CHILDREN, CHILDREN-IN-LAW AND GRANDCHILDREN

When Neelam completed her training to be a doctor at the Medical College of Virginia, she and Andrew were married in a spectacular wedding in Asbury Park in 2001. I do not exaggerate when I say that hundreds of people came.[51] Weddings are central community events in the Hindu culture. Every family member and friend who can be located is invited and comes. In order for Neelam to do a residency in pediatrics, she was required to match with a medical center somewhere in the country. Everywhere she applied, Andrew also applied to the corresponding Master's program in business administration at the same university. So after Neelam was accepted at Emory University in Atlanta and completed her first year, Andrew began the two-year program at Goizueta, Emory's business

---

[51] Although I think I am being fairly accurate, exaggeration and hyperbole are permissible in this book, as they are what I think separate a memoir from an autobiography!

school. When they moved to New Jersey, he began a process of working for several companies that provided medical services. They bought a lovely home in the Wayside section of Ocean Township. In the years that followed, Neelam commuted daily to the Children's Hospital of Philadelphia (CHOP) to do a fellowship in developmental and behavioral pediatrics. She is now a board certified practitioner in this field with a heavy patient load.

For a long time, he had wanted to start his own business. He had thought long and hard about it and had come up with a web-based business called Hipcycle. Hipcycle markets upcycled items. These differ from recycled products in the way they are developed. Recycling is deconstructing products and creating something new. Upcycling is repurposing a product. For example, a bottle becomes a lamp or a tumbler. A fifty-five gallon barrel becomes a composting machine or a soft water rain storage tank. Steve Jobs once said that if you asked a person in 1900 what he wanted for better transportation, he would say a faster horse.[52] Andrew, like Steve Jobs, understands that the future will be populated by people who have a level of imagination that transcends the current vision. He had a great idea that required the selling of his vision and in 2014 Hipcycle was bought out. He has now become an executive at ICIMS, a provider of talent acquisition software solutions for businesses.

Through all of this, Andrew and Neelam produced three stunning children: Aakash, Roshan and Raina. They are, of course, three of the five most wonderful children in the history of the world. Aakash William (named for Daddy Bill) was born

---

[52] From *Steve Jobs, by* Walter Isaacson, Simon and Schuster: New York (2011).

in Atlanta in 2003. We could not get there for the birth. When Roshan was born in New Jersey in 2005, Ellen was invited into the birthing room. Roshan, by the way, is named Roshan James, the fourth James Sell in a row. I am pretty sure I will never know whether he keeps the line alive, but I hope so. We went to Southeast Asia, believing that we would be back before Raina Olivia was born in 2011 in New Jersey, but she beat us to the hospital. They are all great kids. Ellen and I carefully considered what we wanted to be called by our grandchildren. Her mother and grandmother were both called Granny Mac (from MacElrath, their family name). That was not an option, so she proclaimed herself Gege, as in Granny Ellen Granny Ellen. I did not want to be called Grandfather Sell, which my father and his father had seemed to prefer, so I opted for carrying on my mother's father's nickname. He was Papa Hal; I am Papa Jim.

When Katie returned from the Peace Corps, she was in cultural shock. The wealth of the United States does not seem so enormous when you are living within it. But if you are stuck up on an isolated mountain among the poorest of the poor, returning to the United States creates a pretty dramatic contrast. She first took a retail job for the holidays at the MacArthur Mall in Norfolk. She had known of a consulting firm in Washington called Chemonics. They implemented the contractual relationships of the US Agency for International Development (USAID). So if USAID negotiated, say, the reforestation of a Bolivian mountain, Chemonics would make it happen. We had a woman in the church, Andria McClellan, who is bright and experienced in business. I suggested to Katie that she sit down with Andria to learn how to participate in an interview and write a résumé. What a gift Andria was! She gave Katie the confidence she needed to go to Washington and get the job. She also received a strong letter of support from her old boss in El Salvador. Thus, after the first of the year in 2003, Katie moved to Washington and went to work.

While she was there, she decided that she needed to get a Master's degree in international economics. There were several opportunities for such a program in Washington, but she chose the one at American University, because it allowed her to work full-time and go to school full-time, including summer school. She had bought a condo in downtown Washington and for the next year or two, she slogged through that Master's degree and her work requirements at the same time. It must have been a bear. Both jobs had to get done no matter how long they took. As she was finishing up, she learned about a program called the Presidential Management Fellows of the federal government. This program was intended to bring accomplished, career-oriented young people into government service. She applied and was selected among stiff competition. In this program, the fellows would explore a variety of agencies and then select one for their career. She joined the USAID. Because of her prior experience and her selection as a fellow, she did not enter government service anywhere near the bottom rung.

All of her education and experience came together effectively for this career. When President Obama took office, he made international food security his primary diplomatic priority. That work fell right into the lap of her working group. She works directly with multinational corporations seeking to invest in emerging markets through public - private partnerships with the US government, to advance agricultural development. Most of that work is with African nations and in Central America. Most recently, she has also been deeply enmeshed in the U.S. response to the Ebola crisis in Africa.

After some time, she went to a party one night and met a handsome man. A native of Mexico City, Christian Garcia was working for the Mexican embassy as an information technology specialist. He was warm, kind and smart. We kid Katie about what is reported to be her opening comment to Chris: "What do you think of NAFTA?"[53] As her friend and maid of honor, Courtney Pearson likes to say, "That's a line that will snag a guy every time." They seemed well suited for each other and dated for a good while. On one occasion, they went to Rome together, and there, in front of the Coliseum, Christian popped the question. By then, we were living in Annapolis, so it was easy for us to help Katie with her wedding plans. They were married at St. Thomas Church on DuPont Circle by an old friend, Nancy Lee Jose. The reception was at the National Democratic Women's Club. This was during Obama's first presidential campaign in 2008. The place was festooned with campaign banners. My mother must have been cheering from heaven.

Fairly shortly thereafter, they moved out of Katie's little condo on Scott Circle and bought a new one in the Bloomingdale section of Washington. They were shrewd purchasers. This area has become one of the hottest real estate markets in the city. For a long time, Chris had aspired to leave IT behind and become a pastry chef, so he enrolled in La Academe de Cuisine in Maryland. As I write this, he is one of the chefs at "Bread Furst," a highly regarded bakery in Northwest Washington.

---

[53] For "North American Free Trade Agreement".

Then Gege and Papa Jim had a beautiful granddaughter. On August 25, 2010, nine months before her cousin Raina was born, Elena Coco Garcia was born at Washington Hospital Center. Ellen and I were both there. It was wonderful. Katie and Chris speak Spanish to her at home, but she speaks English and Spanish at her preschool program, so she is completely bilingual.

The one whom I am betting is the last of the next generation to make an appearance was Marco Gael Garcia, born on May 17, 2014. Since I knew he was on his way, I held up publication of this story to get him in. The good news, for him, is that he looks a lot like his daddy! The bad news, for him, is that he looks a lot like me!

CHAPTER 9

THE ICING ON THE CAKE

As I said earlier, immediately upon retirement, on May 8, 2005, I left for Florida. One of my aspirations was to find every barbecue restaurant between Norfolk and Florida and sample its wares. I did a good job of that. By that time, Win Lewis had gone to work as the Administrative Assistant to the Bishop of Southern Virginia. The bishop was beyond blessed to have him. Among the jobs in his portfolio was deployment. About twice a year, all the deployment officers up and down the East Coast get together and share suggestions of candidates for vacant parishes. While Win was there, the deployment officer from Maryland announced that he was trying to help the church in Severna Park find an interim rector. He asked if Win had any suggestions. Immediately, Win proposed me and the deployment officer recommended me to Dave Frantz, the Senior Warden of St. Martin's-in-the-Field, Severna Park. Dave was immediately convinced that his church must have me. He instructed a young, energetic attorney, John Poulton, to go after me and not take no for an answer. I had been in Florida for a mere few weeks when John first called. I was flattered to be sought out so aggressively, but I said to him that I was retired. His response was "Well, we could wait until August!" I thought that I had politely turned him down, but I soon discovered that no meant "not right away" to John. As per the warden's instructions, he would not take no for a final answer.

I called Ellen, who was still in Norfolk, and said that maybe this was something I could consider. In 2003, we had sold our home on Westover Avenue and bought a terrific condominium in downtown Norfolk. The neighborhood, West Freemason, was just named one of the top ten neighborhoods in America. By dumb luck, we had bought the Westover property low and sold it at the height of a real estate bubble, so we were able to buy the condo with ample equity. It was purchased to be our retirement home. Ellen was still teaching at Norfolk Academy and finding great satisfaction in her job. We decided that if the position in Severna Park fell together, we might have something of a commuter marriage for a while. She could come up there from time to time and I could slip home. The drive was a little over three hours, and a Southwest Air flight from Norfolk to Baltimore Washington International airport was quick, accessible and affordable.

So I went up to Severna Park and, as I am inclined to do, fell in love with the people and the church. This was while the price of real estate was still going up, so we decided that rather than rent, we would buy a condo in Annapolis. With a little luck, we thought, we could turn around and sell it for a profit when I finished and maybe even end up living there "rent-free". That was the only mistake we made about moving to Annapolis. Shortly after my arrival, the Great Recession fell upon the American economy and there was no way we could sell it. Happily, we have been able to either live in it or rent it as we needed.

St. Martin's-in-the-Field, Severna Park, Maryland

Off and on, over the years, I had thought about ending my career doing interim ministry. Ellen and I both believed that having the opportunity to live in different communities in America might be fun. St. Martin's was going to be my test case. I wanted to see if I was capable of venturing into unknown venues and whether I would enjoy it. I loved every part of it. If people are members of a parish and the rector leaves, they probably find it to be a frustrating proposition to bring in an interim. Businesses rarely operate that way. In most cases, the new CEO is lined up and ready to go when it is time for a change. As I said earlier in this book, in the early 1970s, I followed my predecessor in Lewisburg by one week. It worked fine, so I understand the frustration some people feel when there is a long gap between clergy. However, I served as the interim rector of four different churches and I believe that virtually all of those people will tell you that the time was well spent. Between workshops I gave at the Consortium of Endowed Episcopal Parishes and an article I wrote for a publication called *Vestry Papers*, I was able to clarify what needs to happen in an interim ministry. I put together a list of "thou shalts" and "thou shalt nots" of interim ministry that have become a standard for this niche profession. Without mentioning them all, I will set forth a few of them to illustrate my approach.

1. Thou shalt offer the congregation a new model of ministry that is appropriately different from the past without denigrating that past. Remember that the new

rector will be yet a third model, so you are preparing the way for him or her to live within his or her predilections.

2. Thou shalt do all in your power to create a solid financial ground upon which a new rector can build institutional health.

3. Thou shalt be helpful to the search committee but not nosy. You can answer questions of procedure, process and church etiquette, but their work is none of your business, even if they try to co-opt you.

4. Thou shalt claim no honors. The interim period is not about you. It is about a re-creation of the life and spirit of the congregation. Lavish praise on those who have earned it and be pleased with your self-imposed modesty.

5. Thou shalt honor the fundamentals of ministry: stewardship, worship, adult and children's education, evangelism, outreach and pastoral care. That is a full enough plate.

6. Thou shalt not promote or run down any candidate. Churches are small communities. If you hear rumors, keep them to yourself, or if it is necessary, express yourself to the diocesan deployment officer or bishop. You might learn something that someone needs to know, but it is not your job to interfere.

7. Thou shalt not trash the old rector. Being a rector is not an easy job. Criticism is easy to generate and hard to bury. Indeed, if you can restore the affection of the congregation for the old rector, that can be a blessing to the life of a church in the long run.

8. Thou shalt not dismiss any staff member without due process. Yes, staff members serve at the pleasure of the rector, but you are not the rector. You are the interim. You might think cleaning house while you are the interim is a tradition. It isn't. Yet perhaps some staff members might have to leave. Be sure you know what you are doing and be surrounded by skilled personnel people.

9. Thou shalt not push off onto the congregation a polarizing spiritual or political agenda. There will be people coming out of the woodwork, encouraging you to tell it like it is. That often means "Tell it from *my* perspective, which is way off on the fringe." In these times, it does not take much to upset the delicate balance of church life. Healthy harmony is a virtue when it is honest.

I was at St. Martin's for a year and a half. The church grew strongly and found a new center for its life. During that time, I resurrected a little habit I had engaged in many years earlier. Each Sunday, before each service I would stand outside and welcome worshipers as they came to the door. This accomplished several goals. Of course, it connected me with the entire congregation. Secondly, when I saw newcomers, I could signal a member of the evangelism committee to greet those people and reach out to them. I continued doing it at every church I served. I now wish I had done it everywhere.

Something an interim normally does not engage in is a capital campaign. However, that church had yearned for a new organ for several decades, and when a generous couple offered to put up a considerable amount of money, the vestry encouraged me to apply my fund raising knowledge to the project. Fortunately, all the research had been done on what kind of instrument would fit that church best, so it was simply a matter of presenting a case statement and letting the process take care of itself. We raised the money while we also hired a new organist and redecorated the interior of the church. I was greatly helped in all of this by the young priest who was my assistant, Alistair So. When they called their new rector in 2007, Doris Johnson, she inherited him and a church that was fully alive and ready to receive her.

TRINITY, PRINCETON, NEW JERSEY

I had been an active member of the Consortium of Endowed Episcopal Parishes for more than a dozen years. In that time, I often reconnected with my professional colleague Leslie Smith. The year after I stepped down as an archdeacon, Leslie also left the Diocese of Newark and became the Rector of Trinity Church in Princeton, New Jersey. On several occasions, he and his delegation went out to dinner with my delegation and me at the annual CEEP conference. As a result of that continuing connection, I got to know his Senior Warden, Sylvia Temmer, pretty well. In 2006, Leslie announced that he was going to retire from the active parish ministry. After that announcement, Sylvia contacted me and asked if I would consider being the interim. I made it clear that I could not leave St. Martin's early. It would be inappropriate and unprofessional. We discussed who else might be suitable for that church, but could not come up with the right person.

I had taken four summer Sundays for Leslie when he was on vacation in 2005. There had been a little method to our madness. Roshan James Sell was on his way into the world, just forty-five minutes east of Princeton at Jersey Shore Hospital. I had said to Leslie that I would cover for his vacation if we could stay in the Princeton rectory to be present for Roshan's birth.

Because of that little introduction, not only was I known by Sylvia, but I was also on the radar with the assisting clergy, the organist, some of the staff and a number of members of the vestry. Silvia came back to me and said that if I would consider coming to Trinity upon fulfilling my job at St. Martin's, they would wait for me. They had two full-time assistants who were good and I would probably be only four or five months late. When I proposed this to Ellen, she was happy. After all of her struggles with my moves, this change was a joy from the start. It meant that she could be close to her grandsons in the earliest years of their lives. Being at Roshan's birth bonded her to that boy in deep ways. So she gave the Headmaster of Norfolk Academy plenty of opportunity to find her replacement and retired from teaching after thirty years of service so she could join me in Princeton.

Maybe Princeton is not for everyone, but for Ellen and me, it was abundant happiness. There was nothing about that town and that church that we did not love. Leslie had left it in good shape, as I had known he would. Before he retired, he saw that Sylvia was the Senior Warden and Anne Burns was the Junior Warden. They were both superior. Frank Strasburger was the Associate Rector and Anne Richards was the Curate or Assistant Rector. The organist and choirmaster was Tom Whittemore. I liked them all very much.

The congregation of Trinity Church was an amalgamation of three or four different constituencies. First, there are members of the faculty of Princeton University. I thought they might be intimidating to me. Each of them was a world-class expert in his or her field, but they treated me warmly and generously. They all understood that the church was not the academy. It was the place for nurturing souls, the building of fellowship and a source for healing. I cannot speak for how they were in their classrooms, but in church they were modest, humble and vulnerable. It took me awhile to realize that they treated me like an equal. They were better than good at what they did and they expected the same from me. I did everything within my power not to disappoint them. My preaching, teaching and other ministry was never about living up to some external expectations. It was about reaching down within myself and being as authentic as possible.

A second population was made up of members of the faculty at Princeton Theological Seminary. The university and the seminary are two distinct institutions that, together, comprise a large percentage of Princeton Borough. The largest Protestant seminary in the world, the seminary trains men and women for the Presbyterian ministry as well as many other denominational affiliations. It also has a large postgraduate program offering Master's and Doctoral degrees. The church's property and the seminary's property are contiguous; the university's property begins across the street. We were happily snuggled down in between. Some of the seminary faculty members are Episcopalians. They are there not only because of their scholastic credentials but also because Episcopal students need their mentoring. To have them in the congregation was a delight. They helped out with an occasional program and assisted in other ways when they were invited. Of course, the Episcopalian students who worshiped with us were an enrichment as well. They came from all across America and gave us a continuing breath of fresh air.

This is not to dismiss the faculties, staffs and students of Westminster Choir College, nearby Rutgers University, the amazing Institute for Advanced Study and some extraordinary secondary schools which are all close by. Each of those institutions brought to our door parishioners who enriched us enormously.

But of course, the largest constituency of worshipers was made up of garden-variety human beings who lived in the area and were drawn to the life and ministry of the Episcopal Church. My son likes to say that Princeton is a "bubble." He means that it is a world unto itself. When Albert Einstein arrived there to join the faculty of the Institute for Advanced Study, he was asked what it was like living in Princeton. He said, "Banished to leafy paradise!" In many ways, he was right. For its modest size, it was extraordinarily cosmopolitan. The local newspapers would announce University, Seminary and Institute guest lecturers that the public could attend. We dropped in on them with great frequency, gaining an education in areas that were far outside our usual areas of expertise. We were often invited to the homes of parishioners who were engaged in extraordinary study. The dialogues around those dinner tables were an education unto themselves. Not only was Princeton itself delightful, but also we were an easy train or bus ride to New York City or Philadelphia. We saw a number of Broadway shows while we were there. And of course, our son and his family were less than an hour away; many old

New Jersey friends were within convenient commutes; and our daughter, Katie, was not that far away in Washington, DC.

I was in Princeton for a year and a half. In that time, the church undertook a self-study to gather a sense of where it wished to go in the future. From there, they began a search process that led them to calling a clergyman from Louisville, Kentucky: Paul Jeanes. I remember having the opportunity to talk to him as he was engaged in the matchmaking process. He said to me that he could not have imagined that a place like Trinity would call someone who had spent his whole life in Kentucky. My response was that these people were too secure within themselves to worry about where someone came from. If he could be a person of faith and provide solid leadership, they would accept and appreciate him. He was that kind of person and his ministry there has flourished.

There are many things about Trinity that I love. While I cannot list them all, I must speak of its music program. The organist and choirmaster is Tom Whittemore. He gave me far more credit for my musical knowledge than I deserved. I have always said that I can speak the words of great classic church music far better than I can hum the tunes. The fact of the matter is that after nearly fifty years in the ministry, I still have a relatively limited knowledge of great classical sacred music compared to the music professionals. I have always relied on our choirmasters to give me the guidance I need. What I do have is an experienced ear. After thousands of hours of listening, I can tell the difference between a good music program, an excellent music program, and a superior music program. Tom and his choir were on the upper end of the superior category. Trinity Church is the largest Episcopal

Church north of Washington, DC, and east of Indianapolis. It has the resources to be a model for many ministries. And being closely aligned to nearby Westminster Choir College and the American Boy Choir School, the choirmaster could take advantage of those programs as well. The music program Tom Whittemore had in place there was majestic.

I have to tell you about one amazing service. Every year, on the Sunday between Christmas and New Year's Day, when the student body of Princeton University is on vacation, Trinity would host a service of Christmas Lessons and Carols in the University chapel. The second largest university chapel in America, it holds five thousand people. I introduced to them an old practice that we used in Norfolk. We invited local celebrities to read the nine lessons for the service. On that day, we had Congressman Rush Holt (my all-time favorite congressman and a fellow West Virginian), Noble-Prize-winning economist Dr. Eric Maskin, Bishop George Councell, the President of the American Library Association, the Mayor, the Senior Warden, a local physician in the congregation, a 12-year-old parishioner and our clergy staff to read. Then Tom gathered an orchestra and invited choir alumni who were home for the holidays to join in. In the end, we had over 4,500 worshipers and musicians. It was, by far, the largest congregation in my life!

TRINITY, NEW HAVEN, CONNECTICUT

I finished my work at Princeton in the spring of 2008. However, some time before I left, Tom came by for a visit. He had grown up at Trinity Church, New Haven, Connecticut, and studied under their organist, Walden Moore. The Rector of Trinity, New Haven, Andy Fiddler, had had a long and successful ministry there. Andy and I are the same age, but whereas I served a number of communities, Andy spent almost his entire ministry of more than forty years at Trinity. Tom let me know that Andy was going to announce his retirement for the middle of 2009. He asked if I would be interested in being recommended to their vestry as the interim rector. I was pleased to be considered and the timing was perfect. We had kept our home in Annapolis and we wanted to spend some time with our daughter, Katie, as she prepared to get married to Christian Garcia. Tom offered to talk to Walden, who would be sure to talk to the wardens. So in due course, I was invited and met with Joe Dzeda, the Senior Warden, and Barbara Hedberg, the Junior Warden. Of course, as is the usual circumstance, I fell in love with them. Joe is the curator of organs for Yale University and travels around America restoring Skinner organs. Barbara is a teacher of children who are learning challenged. They both wished the best for their wonderful church.

In August 2009, Ellen and I made our way to New Haven. After considerable exploration, we ended up renting an apartment on the second floor of a classic New England triple-decker. It was in an area that graduate students like to live, called East Rock. Above us lived a wonderful young married couple from Great Britain, Rosie Cole-Hamilton and Guy German. Under us was a succession of other graduate students. We became Rosie and Guy's surrogate parents. Her father is a highly regarded professor at St. Andrew's University in Scotland. Guy is a London boy and former North Sea oil platform engineer doing postdoctoral work in engineering at Yale.

Trinity Church, New Haven, stands at the crossroads of many cultures. Located on the old historic green of New Haven, it is next door to two United Church of Christ (or Congregational) churches, one of which founded Yale University. Therefore, Yale is in the backyard of Trinity Church. Perhaps the people of Yale might say Trinity is in their backyard; it is all a matter of one's perspective! Our front yard was the green. Around the green was a border of streets that formed the central bus transfer station for all New Haven buses. The local lore claimed that an average of two released convicts got off the bus in front of the church every day. The poverty was astounding. And when the pristine elegance of Yale University was juxtaposed with these polyglot people, the area was a case study in urban affairs.

When I arrived, there were two fine assistant rectors: Estelle Webb and Alex Dyer. Estelle was approaching retirement and she ended up retiring less than a year after I arrived. Alex was fresh out of seminary and anxious to have a strong and productive career. Right before I arrived, he launched a ministry on the green for anyone who wanted to come, but especially for the homeless who found a community there. Each Sunday at two o'clock, there was a worship service, followed by lunch. This routine continued fifty-two Sundays a year, no matter what the weather conditions were. Some days, we would have a few dozen attendees. Other days, we would have upward of a hundred. The second winter I was there, it snowed many times over. That never stopped them. (It stopped me...I am too old to worship in a snowstorm.) Yale undergraduates, Yale Divinity School students, and worshipers from other churches joined our street-based parishioners on a regular basis. Throughout the diocese, congregations would bring lunch and help out with the service. Still, today, on Maundy Thursdays, Connecticut's remarkable bishop, Ian Douglas, comes. He washes the feet of the worshipers. That process is followed by a visit from a podiatrist and gifts of fresh shoes and socks. Toward the end of my time there, Alex moved on to another nearby church, but he continued to come back to the Chapel on the Green, with its unique ministry.

I was there for two years. It was a wonderful time, but the first year I needed to begin a gentle process of weaning them away from the nurturing care of Andy Fiddler as they completed renovations to certain areas of their property. The second year saw a sea of change in the church's life. The vestry had undergone a transformation through some successful leadership conferences and they began to look forward. They put together a committee called the by-laws committee. Most churches really do not have by-laws, but the intent was on target. We spent months sorting through what the best practices for the parish should be. Many of the things they had been doing informally were outlined in writing. Policies and procedures from other congregations were studied and adopted as the need arose. As the interim rector, I had no need to have things done my way, but we made the ministry more flexible for the new rector.

A chief defining program of Trinity Church is its music. They budget an unusually high 26 percent of their income on music alone. When I left, there were four distinct choirs. At nine o'clock, they had the Spirit Singers, who sought to lead that service with their informal enthusiasm. The Choir of Men and Girls and the Choir of Men and Boys are both magnificent major choral groups that have national reputations. The men and girls' choir tends to take on a bit more of a lyrical style. The men and boys are a classic Anglican choir that would fit into any British cathedral. Everyone in both the men and girls' choir and the men and boys' choir are paid. Along with their contributions to the worship of the church, they provide excellent training for their young participants. And fourth, the Trinity Singers are a volunteer choir of men and women who sing on a regular basis. In many ways, they are symbolic of the energy that permeates the entire congregation. Since my departure, the Spirit Singers and the Trinity Singers have merged, strengthening both groups.

After more than a year, Alex was nudged by the Suffragan Bishop of Connecticut, Laura Ahrens, to take charge of nearby St. Paul's and St. John's Church (known locally as St. PJ's), located in the wonderful Worcester Square neighborhood about ten blocks away from Trinity. Even though the process for looking for a new rector had already begun, I was able to get Lucy LaRocca to join us for a while. Lucy had just graduated from Yale Divinity School and knew how to hold a sensitive balance between the urban complexities of the New Haven green and the sophistication of Yale. As with most of my other assistants, I knew as soon as I met her that she was the right person for that church. She and I left together when the new rector arrived.

I thought that trying to find the right candidate to be the rector of Trinity Church would be a bigger challenge than it was. I felt that something sacred was going on in that process. Following a long pastorate is hard. Serving an Ivy League community is hard. Serving an urban congregation is hard.

Serving a church that places so much emphasis on music is hard. Finding someone who can hold all of those pieces together is grace. Grace abounds. Somehow, some way, a young priest who had been raised in Belgium, trained as a Roman Catholic in France and then converted to the Episcopal Church found his way to New Haven. The Rev. Luk deVolder is a natural. With a Ph.D. and broad based experience, he has all the skills and energy required for such a place. Trinity ended up in good hands with him.

A symbolic "act of God" that continues to mystify and bring a smile to those who were there, happened on the last day of my term as I was turning matters over to Luk. We awakened that morning after a violent thunderstorm to discover that a substantial corner of the red stone church tower had been struck and fractured by lightning. Pieces of sculpted rock were scattered all over the parking lot. Those who saw the humor in it wondered whether God was saying, "Jim Sell has stayed too long" or "Who let Luk deVolder in?"

Ellen and I enjoyed New Haven. Most days, I would walk to work. A parishioner who made beautiful handmade guitars gave me one. Half way between our home and the church was a music school where I took lessons for a year. We ate out frequently. The restaurants are phenomenal. We would often go over to Yale/New Haven Hospital, where as many as twenty food trucks would be lined up every day, offering an enormous variety of exotic cuisines. Of course, we loved going over to Worcester Square and having what is purported to be the best pizza in America at Sally's or Pepe's. We leaned toward Sally's in the ongoing debate over which is better. Andrew had first put us on to Sally's and Pepe's pizza when he was a student at

Choate. He and some of his buddies would talk a housemaster into driving them down from Wallingford just so they could eat there. I am glad we could follow in his footsteps.

A few days after I arrived in New Haven, Alex wanted to know if I would like to be part of one of the parish's dinner groups. I agreed, provided he put us with some people who were about our age. I will always be appreciative of his matchmaking. Not unlike the other group we had in Sparta, New Jersey, our New Haven dinner group became great friends. To this day, we stay in contact with them. One of the basic reasons we agreed to move to Connecticut was because we wanted to reconnect with my old high school friends Frank and Liz Kirkpatrick in Hartford and Chet and Evelyn Shuman in Boston. We saw the Kirkpatricks a lot. Having the Shumans and Kirkpatricks come down for the Harvard-Yale football game was an iconic moment. Together, the six of us sojourned back to Charleston for out fiftieth high school reunion, where I preached the Sunday morning sermon. Meanwhile, Leslie and Lois Smith ended up in nearby Stonington, Connecticut, where he was the interim and we continued our lifelong game of tag while we were all there.

Believing that my career as an interim was over, Ellen and I said good-bye to Trinity, East Rock, New Haven, Yale and many good friends and headed back to Norfolk.

EASTERN SHORE CHAPEL, VIRGINIA BEACH, VIRGINIA

We arrived back in Norfolk in late June 2011. We were kind of keeping a low profile while I played golf with Lee Georges and were just getting re-oriented to our home. On one occasion about six months into our arrival, Ellen went to our local grocery store. On the street that backs up to that store is the home of the Rev. Sue Crommelin and her husband, Paul Dell. Sue was our Spiritual Director at Christ and St. Luke's and one of those wonderful parishioners who was nudged into going to seminary somewhat late in life. Ellen and I both admire her greatly. After graduating from the Episcopal Divinity School in Cambridge, Massachusetts, she had served at Trinity, Portsmouth, and at that moment, was an assistant at Eastern Shore Chapel, Virginia Beach. She came out of her house, looked up, saw Ellen and said, "Oh my! You and Jim are back. Eastern Shore Chapel is looking for an interim."

That evening, Sue and I talked. I learned that their rector, Chris Thompson, had retired some months earlier and had moved to, of all places, Lewisburg, West Virginia. While looking for a traditional interim, Sue and the other two assistants had held down the fort. Then one of those assistants had also retired and now Sue and the remaining assistant, James Medley, were left. Sue was strictly part-time and James was just a few years out of seminary. They were in a tight spot.

A day or two later, I received a phone call from Edwin Brown, the Senior Warden, and Susan Buchanan, the Junior Warden, who asked if I would consider a possible interim ministry. I was positively disposed, if for no other reason than because I could sleep in my own bed in my own home. The church was only about twelve miles down the interstate from where we lived. We had a lively and mutually supportive conversation that led to an interview with the full vestry. Eastern Shore Chapel (ESC) is a church that I have known of for nearly twenty-five years. The rector who was there when I was in Norfolk, Andy MacBeth, was a talented man whom I considered a friend. A historic church with its roots in colonial Virginia, it has a name that is misleading on several levels. First of all, it is not on the eastern shore of Virginia, but it was, in its first iteration, on the eastern shore of the Lynnhaven River. Historically, it was a "chapel of ease" for members of the much older Old Donation Episcopal Church nearby, [54] hence its name of Chapel. By today's definitions, we think of a chapel as some quaint little rural edifice. In fact, ESC is neither quaint nor little. It consists of the largest church building complex I ever served. During the heyday of church growth, new additions kept being added to their property, making it into an extensive campus. They own thirty-two acres of land, including a cemetery. Their ministries include a large day school, a bookstore and an extensive outreach program. Their Chapel Pantry, which is run out of the old rectory, provides groceries to hundreds of people per month. Every day, there is at least one self-help ministry, such as AA, offered. A full catalogue of worship services, Bible studies, prayer groups and other spiritual programs fill the weekly calendar. Trinity, New Haven, had its offices on the sixth floor of a downtown office building. We rarely had anyone drop in, so the fact that about three hundred to five hundred people walked onto ESC's campus each day was a joy to behold for one obsessed with numbers.

---

[54] *Chapel of ease* was a colonial term for an adjunct church building under the administration of a parish church. It was constructed within a short carriage ride of a group of parishioners to ease their attendance on Sunday mornings.

When I told them they had fewer problems than the other churches I had served in the recent past, they thought I was exaggerating. They had gone through a long period of slow decline in attendance and they had begun to give up on themselves. They were convinced that "no one who was any good" would want to come to their church as a new rector. The fact of the matter is that they were and are a thriving congregation. It is true that in their quest for new members, other churches circled about them like vultures, picking off the low-hanging fruit of their inactive members. And there was definitely a thinning gap in the critical twenty-five to forty-five-year-old population, but that was all surmountable. This church had all the makings of a great parish. My task was simple: I merely had to help them redefine their vision and identity as a spiritual community in Virginia Beach, Virginia. From an objective point of view, I could see that they are the most balanced mainline Episcopal congregation in the heart of the largest city in the state of Virginia. They pride themselves on their positions of inclusivity for LGBT citizens. They honor the widest variety of spiritual journeys while holding tightly to the faith of Jesus Christ. Some of the larger Protestant churches in Virginia Beach seem to have a polarized and narrow view of what it means to be a Christian. Any open-minded searcher would discover that Eastern Shore Chapel abounds in the kind of gracefulness that people yearn to be a part of.

When I first met with the staff, they were so anxious that they begged the Senior Warden to be in attendance. I cannot imagine what they thought I was, but some of them were suspicious of me before I showed up. Happily, we got through that distress in a mere few hours and were on our way to rebuilding the church. It is a remarkable staff that any church would envy. As I have said, Sue Crommelin-Dell is a gifted spiritual director and pastoral presence. James Medley is a diamond; not a diamond in the rough but a highly polished gem. Before my eyes, I watched him bloom into a talented preacher and liturgist. I found that I could count on him to be the kind of pastor that church required. If there was a medical emergency or pastoral issue, he would be there in a heartbeat. The remainder of the large staff all brought unique and special gifts to their individual positions. They are a curious lot, all uniquely talented but all very different. Andy MacBeth had hired most of them and he had done a good job.

I was happy that I could end my full-time parish ministry at ESC. I felt comfortable there. I was not a bit surprised when they called a rector who seemed as if he came from central casting. The Rev. Tom Deppe had been a lay member back in the 1980s, when he was in the US Navy as a pilot stationed at nearby Oceana Naval Air Station. He then went to the Seminary of the Southwest in Austin, Texas. From there, he served in Mississippi and Jacksonville, Florida. It is like coming home for him.

So finally, I packed up my stoles and vestments and drove back up Interstate 264 to our wonderful condominium by the Pagoda and *Battleship Wisconsin* in Norfolk. Forty-four years have flown by. My heart is still passionate about life in the ministry. However, I do not miss the evening meetings or the 6:00 a.m. Sunday alarms. And from now on, I will never miss another Christmas morning with a grandchild! Maybe sometime, I will stay up and watch *Saturday Night Live*, a pleasure that was never available to me. Or maybe not.

SUMMING UP

Somewhere in the height of my panic attacks over the prospect of dying, I made a decision. Rather than obsess over the coming of my death, I would be somewhat like a member of Alcoholics Anonymous and take life one day at a time. It was clear that I had no control over when I died, but I could have some control over my living. I could squeeze out as much life as possible from each day. I do not believe anyone goes to hell, so I did not have to worry about whether I qualified for God's love. God's love was a freely given grace that I could enjoy and be thankful for. So I adopted another agenda: I came to love the fabric of living. Of course, some days were not fun. On many occasions, I did the wrong thing, spoke stupid words or let down the people I loved the most. But through it all, I had only one objective. On the last day of my cognitive life, I wanted to be able to say, in total truthfulness, "Oh God. How I loved it all. How I loved my wife. How I loved my children and their spouses and children. How I loved my family far and near. How I loved my calling and my responsibilities. How I loved the churches I was privileged to serve. How I loved my friends. How I loved living every day. How I loved the opportunity to learn to live."

I have lived in wonderful places, met thousands upon thousands of amazing people and had experiences I never imagined would be mine. I aspired to a life of tender mercies. I got that, plus I received traveling mercies that a little boy from West Virginia was sure he would never receive.

While I have hoped I would be blessed with a long, abundant and healthy life, I recognized that the proverbial tractor-trailer truck could blow me away at any moment. So every night, rather than pray the prayer of death I was taught as a child,[55] I have called out to God and said, "Oh God, I loved it."

---

[55] "Now I lay me down to sleep. I pray the Lord my soul to keep. But if I should die before I wake, I pray the Lord my soul to take. Amen."

A Concluding Sermon

I was an itinerant tradesman: a journeyman. I would come into a town with my knapsack filled with the tools of my trade, and I would set about doing the job the union and the company assigned me.

But time is the great shop foreman. My shift has drawn to a close. The hour has arrived for me to punch out on the time clock. Even when my heart says, "Stay a little," I know it is time for me to gather my tools and turn to leave.

My tools are few. They fit neatly in my knapsack. They are joy, memory, faith, hope, love, intuition, metaphor, tolerance and passion: not much else. As I gather them, I look for signs of wear. In some strange way, these tools seem to have been more finely honed through my use.

I look around as I pack, and I have an idea. I decide to reach around and gather a few treasures. I will snitch some recollections that I can stuff in and save like the pearls of great price that they are.

The most valuable gifts I accumulated are the people I met. I did not have any parishioners. I had only friends; people who shared with me an insight, a laugh, a tear, a journey. We have been bound together. They gave me their hearts and let me peer into their souls. I stash their love in my knapsack. I will take it with me to treat like the precious treasure it is. I have been enriched by their hope, faith and integrity.

I was blessed with an abundant ministry because of the many people I counted as colleagues. From the earliest days, when I just had a part-time secretary and a poorly paid or volunteer organist, to the robust years, when we had hot and cold running clergy and support staffs that tended to the widest range of parochial responsibilities, I was surrounded by wonderful people who believed in the mission of their church and always tried to give their best.

As I punch out on the time clock, the shop steward demands an accounting. Have the company's policies and procedures been adhered to? I stop, ponder and wonder. Somehow, I know something about myself. It probably looks like smugness to those on the outside, but it is actually the opposite: it is raging humility. I received such unmerited grace in that I dwelled among a series of churches that were always at the top of their game when I was there.

What were those policies and procedures the company built its identity upon? The words are simple yet profound. The calling of each of those churches was to be an inclusive community of Christian journeyers who honored the wide boundaries of human spirituality. They sought to be well-grounded in affairs of the Spirit and they all expected transforming worship, inspired preaching, excellent education, authentic evangelism, broad-based outreach, sensitive pastoral care and faithful stewardship.

They expected better than good preaching. I was welcome to plumb the depths of my personal faith. They would never tolerate trite or unimaginative preaching. They expected honesty, intelligence, sophistication and spiritual maturity.

When it came to the art of Christian formation, they expected programs that were not so much about learning facts as they were about sharing in the friendship of people who aspired to a life of faith. There are always new questions to be asked and new discoveries to be made in the ongoing saga of mature spiritual growth.

Beautiful worship and music is fundamental. People want to go to church to come into contact with the rapture of God's in-breaking glory. The churches I served were blessed with abundant musical and liturgical talent. They were not afraid to try promising things, adventure into new experiences and model creativity and excellence, while they held on to the brilliance found in classic Anglican norms. They constantly raised the bar on the standards for excellence.

What is real outreach? A church that does not listen to the baptismal covenant to "respect the dignity of every human being" is a church that is flawed at its core. Outreach is not primarily about throwing around money with lavish generosity. The purpose of an outreach ministry is for every single man, woman, and child in the church to throw love around with lavish generosity. It is about breaking the sociological, cultural and spiritual barriers that separate us as peoples, tribes and clans.

"No one is an island. None of us stand alone."[56] To be a human being is to live in a community. Churches can be training grounds for learning to take care of others. Attendance increased in all the churches I served - some many times over. The churches that grew the most on my shift were the ones

---

[56] From John Donne, "Meditation XVII," *Devotions upon Emergent Occasions* (1624).

that had a natural proclivity for personal pastoral care and a welcoming heart. Church members have no business being standoffish or unwelcoming. The world yearns for what healthy, open-minded Episcopal churches offer and it simply must be shared.

As I turn away, I can now reveal a truth that I have kept somewhat secret most of the time: I do not know what individuals gave to their parishes. I wanted them to think I did, because attention to details is important and giving is a major responsibility of the rector. Where a person's treasure is spent reveals everything about his or her values, but in the end, stewardship is not about arithmetic. Stewardship is about loving the church of Jesus Christ with all your heart and soul and might and mane. Giving is one of the greatest joys of living, and giving to one's church is a proclamation that "all good gifts of love are sent from heaven above."[57]

And as I buckle up my knapsack, I can affirm that my time in the clergy union has given me a deep perspective. I have the capacity to cast an eye into the heart of any Episcopal congregation. What they do is serious business. We are a church called to preach and proclaim the gospel of Jesus Christ. We are not some secret society or social club. We are not a sect of dithering fundamentalists who drift off into single issue exclusivity. We never think we have all the answers to life's gravest questions. Most of the time we are little more than faith-filled agnostics. We are called to be of a gentle and modest heart, knowing that God's will is grounded in love and that we are all loved beyond our wildest expectations. We are called to model, for the broader communities that surround us, an

---

[57] Hymn by Johann P. Schultz (1800).

attitude of honoring all sorts and conditions of people. There are no litmus tests or scorecards in God's love. In heterogeneity, we grow and live an enriching life. We must proclaim that every spiritual journey is of God and there are as many pathways to heaven as there are individuals engaged in the adventure. As far as I can tell, this is the primary Episcopal mission in the twenty-first century. I see no other institution that is better equipped to do it.

The work of the Episcopal Church and all the policies and procedures of the shop steward come down to one thing: our objective is to help people see themselves as the saints they are, dwelling in the radiant love of God, no matter what our spiritual history. Knowing that we are saints is an invitation to live extravagantly happy lives.

The steward asks about my wages. I am paid in full. My payoff is that I will always be standing beside each worshiper I ever served as his or her spiritual friend. We have lived a life together as sister and brother in Christ. Now the journey continues for each of us. I hoist my pack upon my shoulders. My journey is about to take me down some new paths, but we are forever bonded to one another. What generous payment for hired labor. Amen.

ACKNOWLEDGMENTS

A number of people have honored me by reading this text to look for egregious errors in fact and to make suggestions as to style and perspective. I am deeply indebted to them; however, in no way are they held accountable for my sins and omissions. Those readers are Ellen Sell, Andrew Sell, Katie Garcia, Frank Kirkpatrick, Liz Kirkpatrick, Chet Shuman, Len Freeman, Lindsay Freeman, Jo Helen DePue, Sue Crommelin-Dell, Win Lewis, Greg Johnson, Bob Turoff and Sylvia Temmer. I am deeply appreciative. Whatever quality one might find in these words is the direct result of their critiques.

I am especially indebted to Dr. Leon-Paul Georges, retired US Navy physician, endocrinologist, founder of the Strelitz Diabetes Institutes of the Eastern Virginia Medical School, my golfing friend and adversary and watercolor artist extraordinaire who painted the evocative painting on the cover of this book.

I am equally indebted to Ricks S. Voight, perhaps the finest photographer I have ever known, who made the picture on the back of this book. I promise you that I am not nearly as handsome as he has made me look.

Appendix 1

St. Patrick's Breastplate

There is ample evidence that St. Patrick wrote this piece of poetry in the fifth century, although some scholars think it might have been substantially edited several hundred years later. It is usually referred to as St. Patrick's Breastplate. There are a number of versions extant. This is from *The Episcopal Hymnal* (hymn 370). I sang it at my ordinations. I sing it every chance I get. I think of it as my creed.

> I bind unto myself today the strong Name of the Trinity, by invocation of the same, the Three in One, and One in Three.

> I bind this day to me forever, by power of faith, Christ's Incarnation; his baptism in Jordan River; his death on cross for my salvation; his bursting from the spiced tomb; his riding up the heavenly way; his coming at the day of doom: I bind unto myself today.

I bind unto myself the power of the great love of cherubim; the sweet "Well done" in judgment hour; the service of the seraphim; confessors' faith, apostles' word, the patriarchs' prayers, the prophets' scrolls; all good deeds done unto the Lord, and purity of virgin souls.

I bind unto myself today the virtues of the starlit heaven the glorious sun's life-giving ray, the whiteness of the moon at even, the flashing of the lightning free, the whirling wind's tempestuous shocks, the stable earth, the deep salt sea, around the old eternal rocks.

I bind unto myself today the power of God to hold and lead, his eye to watch, his might to stay, his ear to hearken, to my need; the wisdom of my God to teach, his hand to guide, his shield to ward; the word of God to give me speech, his heavenly host to be my guard.

Christ be with me, Christ within me, Christ behind me, Christ before me, Christ beside me, Christ to win me, Christ to comfort and restore me. Christ beneath me, Christ above me, Christ in quiet, Christ in danger, Christ in hearts of all that love me, Christ in mouth of friend and stranger.

I bind unto myself today the strong Name of the
Trinity, by invocation of the same, the Three in
One, and One in Three. Of whom all nature hath
creation, eternal Father, Spirit, Word: praise to
the Lord of my salvation, salvation is of Christ
the Lord.

Words attributed to St. Patrick (372–466). Translated by Cecil
Frances Alexander (1818–1895) in 1889.

Appendix 2

The Christmas Hymn

James W. H. Sell

The village streets are dark and still; the winter night is mild.
The earth, in lonely vigil, lies with dreams of heaven's child.
The breath of God divides the sky and stirs the angel's wings;
They fly to every longing soul, proclaiming wondrous things.

The stars are flung like diamonds white, across creation's roof,
To guide the princes of the realm and shepherds to the truth
That to that lonely cattle stall, a pathway has been led.
For Christ our Lord is born for us, a manger for his bed.

Come see the holy mystery of God's incarnate love.
Amidst the straw and swaddling clothes, the splendor from
    above.
The promise of unending joy upon the maiden's breast.
In beauty and ascending awe, the blessed babe at rest.

And suddenly, the world breaks forth in praises to the King;
All tribes and nations, castes and clans, united voices sing
Of faith redeemed and hope renewed within this humble home:
The glory of the Christ glows bright for journeyers to come.

I composed this in 1995 while I was attending the Stephen Ministry training. It has had a few minor adjustments over the years. There have been several musical settings for it. The one by Agnes Wynne in 2012 is the most recent.

10-6-15